TWO FOR TH

Two for the Road

Travel tales by

Anita Feleo &
David Sheniak

Two for the Road
Anita Feleo and David Sheniak

Published and exclusively distributed by
ANVIL PUBLISHING, INC.
2/F Team Pacific Building
13 Jose Cruz St.
Barrio Ugong, 1604 Pasig City
Philippines
Telephone: 914.0155

The National Library of the Philippines CIP Data

Recommended entry:

Feleo, Anita.
Two for the road: travel tales/
by Anita Feleo and David Sheniak.-
Pasig City : Anvil Pub., c1998
1 v

1. Philippine essays (English).
2. Voyages and travels. I. Sheniak, David.
II. Title.

PL5546E 1997 899.21'04 P973000067
ISBN 971-27-0647-8

Cover and interior design by MANNI CHAVES
Pen and ink art by BO CUMAGUN

Printed in the Philippines

AUTHORS' NOTE

A man standing on a beach sees a different ocean from minute to minute. Although it may seem the same, it is forever changing. Likewise, the traveler can never see the same destination twice. Even though the words most often found in travel books are "timeless" and "eternal," in truth, places too are always changing, presenting new aspects of themselves for discovery. Every location is fresh, different and exciting no matter how many times you have been there before.

It is the passion of the travel writer to bring this excitement to the printed page. *Two For The Road* is a chronicle of the changing Philippine landscape, the people who populate it and the different faces they wear.

We hope that through these stories you come to see some familiar places with a new eye, learn about other places you might never have heard of before, and meet some very interesting people along the way... the best reasons to travel.

Contents

Introduction

PERHAPS THE first travel book ever written was the Bible. After all, a good part of it chronicles the wanderings of the early Jews through Canaan, Egypt and the Holy Land, and later of Jesus and his disciples over much the same territory. In Acts 27 and 28, for example, we read a recounting, in vivid detail, of St. Paul's return to Rome, a violent journey across the Mediterranean which ended in a shipwreck:

> 27:41 And falling into a place where two seas meet [*Mediterranean* and *Ionian Seas*], they ran the ship aground; and the forepart stuck fast, and remained unmovable, but the hinder was broken with the violence of the waves.
>
> 27:43 But one centurion, willing to save Paul, kept the others [*centurions*] from their purpose [*to kill the prisoners*] and commanded that they which could swim should cast themselves first into the sea and get to land.
>
> 28:1 And when they were escaped, then they knew that the island was called Melita [*Malta*].
>
> 28:2 And the barbarous people shewed us no little kindness: for they kindled a fire, received us every one, because of the present rain and because of the cold.

The rest of the chapter follows St. Paul's discontinuous sea voyage from Malta, through Syracuse, to Alexandria and finally Rome. The chapter could easily have been written by some ancient travel writer.

Long before the time of St. Paul, in 5th century B.C., Homer wrote about Odysseus' travels around the same Mediterranean and fifteen centuries later Paul Theroux followed in the Ithacan king's footsteps and recorded his journey in the *Pillars of Hercules.*

Closer to home, the ancient narrative, *Maragtas,* recalls the voyage of ten Bornean *datus* who fled their homeland in the 13th century to escape tyranny. Tide and wind brought them first to Panay Island and then to the Visayas and Luzon, which they would explore and settle. The tale, handed down from generation to generation through oral tradition, is an early attempt to link the Philippines with the great Southeast Asian island-world.

UNTIL TELEVISION upstaged the printed word, travel books were people's principal doorway to the exotic. As early as 1296, Marco Polo brought the mysteries and splendors of far-off Cathay to European readers. That much of his book is now considered exaggeration—in fact revisionist historians are doubting that he ever went to Mongolia—didn't reduce its immense popularity or its importance at the time. It was the accepted account of life in China for almost 600 years until new voyages and new travel books corrected Europe's earlier impressions.

In the 15th century, during the Age of Exploration, the great adventurers either kept journals or took a chronicler with them. Thus their patrons and fellow countrymen who could read were rewarded with amazing stories, like *A Journal of the First Voyage of Vasco Da Gama* by a G. Corea and *The Travels of Hernando De Soto* by an author known only as a Gentleman of Elvas.

The early Europeans also learned about a strange group of Pacific islands now known as the Philippines through the journals of Antonio Pigafetta, who traveled with Magellan. One could almost experience Pigafetta's excitement as he describes the first encounter between Magellan and Raja Colambu:

> **The ruler of Cebu received us in his bamboo palace, seated on a mat, draped in gold and precious gems, nibbling at turtle eggs served on a porcelain plate, while being entertained by women dancing to the music of brass gongs and drums.**

By the 1800s, European curiosity about the far-off Philippines was being sated by priests and traders who were regularly bringing back stories of the islands, from urbane Manila to the "savage" Cordilleras.

Anticipating Masferre's and Scott's chronicles of the Ifugao, Paul Proust de la Geronier, a French doctor, wrote his own journal about the northern provinces, *Twenty Years in the Philippines*. Although his language is a bit rough in places, Geronier was a keen observer, albeit with all his "old world" prejudices intact:

> I wished, if possible, to make an excursion to the Tinguians and Igorots, wild populations, who were much talked of, but little known... My amazement was very great when I beheld tall men, and really handsome elegant women. Was I really among savages? The only clothing the men wore was a sash and some sort of turban made out of bark from the fig tree. They were armed, as they always are, with a long spear, a small hatchet and a shield. The women also wore a sash, and a small narrow apron that came down to their knees. Their heads were ornamented with pearls, coral beads, and pieces of gold, twisted among their hair; the upper parts of their hands were painted blue.

Another remarkable chronicler of the Philippines was Feodor Jagor, a German historian and scientist who visited the islands in 1860. Not only did he keep his own journals, he also collected and published the works of earlier visitors. The following is an eyewitness account of Mt. Mayon's eruption in 1816, which almost destroyed the Bicol region, as told by Fr. Francisco Tubino and recorded by Jagor:

> The volcano appeared black at its base, darker higher up, variegated in the middle, and on the peak an ashen color While contemplating this spectacle we felt a violent earthquake followed by a strong thunder. The mountains spewed forth lava with great force and the cloud that crowned it generally increased. The ground became dark, the air was lit up; rays and sparks could be seen emerging from the mountain, forming a horrible tempest. Immediately there started a rain of large and incandescent carbonized stones that set fire to anything they touched and consumed it;

shortly thereafter, smaller stones, sand and ashes fell. This did not stop in three hours, the obscurity lasted about five. The towns of Camalig, Cagsaua, Baudiao and half of Albay and Guinobatan were set on fire and destroyed.

WHILE THE world is definitely getting smaller, travel books can still be doorways to new experiences. Unlike the filmed travelogue which creates a quick record of a destination, the travel book moves more slowly, pacing itself as the traveler does, taking the time to offer the reader the author's personal experiences and insights. Storytellers like Peter Mayle, Norman Lewis, Paul Theroux and Pico Iyer allow you to share in their adventures, sometimes in extraordinary locales, other times in very familiar settings. It is like looking at the world through a different set of eyes. Many of Graham Greene's readers have been to Paris, but not with Henry's Aunt Augusta.

LIKE OTHER restless chroniclers, we have been moving around the globe most of our adult lives and traveling in the Philippines for nearly a decade. *Two For The Road* is the personal journal of our Philippine trips from 1991 to 1996.

Right from the very beginning we decided we wanted to avoid upscale resorts and deluxe hotels as much as possible. Places that cater to international tourists seem to lose their cultural identity or rather create a new one called "five-star standard." Like McDonald's, a Hyatt or a Club Med looks the same anywhere in the world. They may be located in a particular country but they never become part of that country. Sometimes they are so self-contained you expect to see signs reminding their guests what particular part of the world they're in.

Instead we planned our Philippine trips via the *carinderias*, beer houses, museums, festivals, towns and villages from Batanes to Davao. We didn't find many Beautiful People but rather a lot of beautiful people. *Two For The Road* is populated with ordinary men and women who have opened their hearts and their homes to us. We have tried to record faithfully their stories and their lives. In "A Faraway Nest" you will meet a town founder who is struggling to preserve his town's heritage, and in "A Negros Safari" another town founder is struggling to remember her own. In other places in the book you will see a moviehouse in a fishing town decorated by Cecil B. DeMille, encounter a French couple who went native at a birthday party, find out how a group of young architects are trying to save a town, and fly with a pilot who has turned back the clock 50 years.

Traveling is also discovery. We were able to see how a province prepared for the Lenten season and wrote about it in "Rites Before The Rites." In "Out of Africa" we found a displaced continent. Sometimes what you discover when traveling are just your own impressions. "Phoenix Rising," "Speculation On A Neighborhood Enigma," "Bohol In The Rain" and "Being There" are musings on some familiar locations. "Above and Below Ground In Palawan" are thoughts about a place as alien as the moon.

WHENEVER ON the road, we try to look for that something that makes a place different. And most of the time we find it. But we have also discovered that the differences which set places apart are not as compelling as the similarities that bind them together. Whether in Luzon, Visayas or Mindanao, Filipinos laugh over the same things, dream the same dreams and hope for the same things. *Two For The Road,* we hope, captures these.

Luzon

A visit to another world

BA-TAN-ES. Three syllables that conjure the distant, the forbidding, the beautiful—and a challenge to serious travelers.

We have made two trips to Batanes so by now you would think that for us it is a familiar destination. Not really. Even today, should we go there for the third time (and we hope we do), we still would not have a clue as to how things might turn out. All we could be certain of is that we would be heading for a place measured less by the rod than by psychic distance, where beauty can be, as Rilke puts it, "the beginning of Terror."

The Batanes Archipelago lies on the northernmost tip of the Philippines where the Pacific Ocean meets the China Sea at a treacherous expanse of water called the Balintang Channel. It is only 525 miles from Manila, but it may as well be another world.

Batanes is the Philippines' smallest province both in area (21,099 hectares) and population (14,663). It is made up of three islands, Batan, Sabtang and Itbayat, and seven islands including Y'ami, where on a clear day, the folk say you can see Formosa. They also like to say that they are closer to that Chinese island than they are to Manila. In fact, radio broadcasts from Formosa are clearer than those beamed from Tuguegarao.

Batan, the largest island, contains the capital town of Basco. Sabtang is a boat ride away from Batan, across the Balintang Channel. Itbayat is less accessible. Not only is it reined in by towering cliffs that drop sharply to the sea, there is no pier or beach anywhere. Strong currents prevent boats from ferrying commuters regularly to this island, and there is a technique to getting on and off shore. To go ashore, you have to wait for a strong wave to thrust the boat up to ground level then jump off. You execute the same acrobatic feat to climb aboard.

In Batanes, the sea is ever present. It locks horns with limestone rocks, crashes onto shores and, in Vulugan, further polishes the smooth stones covering the beach. It never rests, and the irony is, with all this water around you can never go for a swim. In constant motion, the sea spews white caps that form long, foamy, horizontal lines from the horizon to the shore. This is on clear days. On bad days the sea becomes a roiling monster, heaving waves that crest at thirty feet. Then, like a bulldozer run amok, its rushing waters pick up boulders as big as houses from the sea floor and send them hurtling onto rooftops ashore. Entire villages have been buried under sand and rocks. And substantial fishing boats have been tossed around like toys or carried away to nowhere, never to be seen again. It is not surprising that most families have lost at least one member to the sea.

If the sea is unpredictable, the hills are a constant. Up in what folk call "Marlboro County," you sort of expect to see a tattooed cowboy light up as he surveys his herd of cattle from the saddle. Or a squeaky clean Julie Andrews to materialize singing a paean to the Kodakchrome panorama.

Between the sea and the hills, on narrow strips of flatter land, is where the people live, in squat stone houses that hug the earth, as immovable and traditional as the inhabitants themselves.

WHILE PLANNING our first trip to Batanes in 1988, everyone we knew had only one thing to say: "We'll see you when we see you." Even the ticketing clerk at the PAL office wouldn't confirm our departure or arrival date. It depends on the weather, was her curt reply.

Air travel is the only means of transportation to Basco. The town's only other contact with the rest of the country is via the navy, which sends a boat there two or three times a year—depending upon the weather—to bring in heavy supplies. While PAL flies daily to Basco, it does so only on good days. A mere drizzle or a slight rise in wind velocity is sufficient reason to declare *force majeure* and the flight is immediately canceled.

In Batanes, a perfectly sunny day could turn, without warning, into a waterlogged nightmare. There is always a wind, a shower every afternoon and frequently typhoons, especially from July to October. In the winter months (December to February), the temperature can go down as low as 7°C.

However, the notion that Batanes is continually battered by typhoons is a myth. Batanes is always mentioned in connection with weather disturbances simply because Basco contains the last weather station in the north and is thus a point of reference for all typhoons that enter the Philippines. However, when a typhoon does come, it hits the province with a force that can break the barometer.

Forewarned and forearmed, we took our chances: we figured if something did happen, it would make better copy. In fact, our photographer and friend, Sonny Yabao, was secretly hoping for a typhoon. "Imagine what great pictures that would make," he told us later, recalling the visual impact of "Monsoon," a photo essay shot by a colleague for *Life*.

FROM THE air, as our Fokker 50 glided down the runway at the foot of Mount Iraya, we watched the pastoral hills roll down to a savage sea where indifferent birds rode the high waves. Puffs of foliage of the deepest green peeped out of the vast meadows. Tall grass bent to the wind's way. A rainbow, with its fragile promise of better weather, held back the low clouds. The morning sun swaddled the land with golden light. It was a beautiful day in Basco.

We alighted from the plane to cheerful applause. "Is there a celebrity on board?" we asked the stewardess. "No," she said, "just us." Apparently, the folk of Basco have made a ceremony of meeting and seeing off every flight. As soon as they hear the plane's engines overhead, they rush to the airport, form an impromptu welcoming committee arranged in semi-circle several persons deep with the small children in front, and applaud a successful landing. Every passenger is greeted with a broad smile, more so if he or she is a homecoming native son or daughter.

After collecting our baggage, we asked around for a taxi to town. The man we put the question to was apologetic. "No cabs here," he said smiling shyly, "but you can take a tricycle or walk." The town was just at the end of the airport road, he assured us, and he was right. Before we could feel the weight of our bags we were at the gate of Mama Lily, Basco's only inn, and our home for the next four days.

We quickly learned that Batanes doesn't lend itself to tourism as we know it. For one, moving around is strictly by foot power. Those who could afford them tooled around on motorcycles or bicycles; everybody else walked and considered hoofing seven kilometers nothing special.

There were no televisions, movie houses, shopping malls or restaurants, although Mama Lily served its boarders delicious meals. In Basco, electricity was shut off after seven, and we found little to do to pass the evenings. Not surprisingly, the province's alcohol consumption (including our own) by the governor's admission, was highest in the country. But although life was hard, nobody locked their doors or windows—except during a typhoon.

So what did we do in Batanes? We let the place come to us at its own pace. The governor lent us a jeep, and we could have circled Batan in two hours, but we wanted more than a ride-through. So we inched our way, at 20 kph, to savor the quaint towns of Mahatao, Ivana and Uyugan, as well as the picturesque meadows and in-land seas that can be found all over the island.

We were lucky to be there in October, the month of processions in honor of the Virgin. Unlike elsewhere in the Philippines, the religious procession in Batanes does away with candles (no candle could hold up to the wind). Neither is it attended with pomp.

October is also the month of the *kuyab*, migratory birds from China that come to roost in Batanes in flocks of hundreds a day or so before they continue their southward flight to warmer climes. The *kuyab*, the folk claim, are the Virgin's birds for they never fail to show up on October 13 every year, alighting on treetops and keeping their perch until the Virgin's procession passes by.

This October 13, the *kuyab* didn't show up. Not in Mahatao or any other Batanes town. The folk were disappointed—so were we—and put the blame on changing weather patterns. Yet the procession went on as scheduled. It was the most solemn we've seen. Old women in white blouses and black skirts wore scapulars with the Virgin's face. Surprisingly, their heads were covered with black veils, a Roman Catholic accessory that we thought had gone the way of the Latin Mass. Young girls, dressed in white like first communicants, strew flower petals on the Virgin's path, while old men still agile at the violin played obscure hymns.

Everything proceeded quietly. Now and then the constantly moving air stirred the old women's veils and rustled the yellowed music sheets. But no matter how hard the wind blew, the prayers and songs rode a decibel above its howl as if proclaiming the triumph of faith over the elements.

During the procession we noticed an old priest, a Biblical archetype with a touch of Rasputin. We approached him later to talk to him, but he shooed us away. "I have nothing to say," he barked in his Spanish-accented English, waving his bony fingers at us. "He is from the Canary Islands," a teacher we met told us, "and he is not too friendly these days. But he is a good priest." We learned the priest spent most of his missionary days in Itbayat and had come to Mahatao to retire. Now we thought we understood his curtness. Perhaps in his youth he burned with religious zeal. But living in a place God seems to have forsaken was probably too much even for an ascetic to bear.

THE IVATAN, the natives of Batanes, trace their roots to prehistoric Formosan immigrants and Spanish conquistadors. Basco carries the name of the Castillan who brought the province under Spanish rule in 1788 and who served as its first governor-general.

Unlike most Filipinos who emerge from an eclectic gene pool through intermarriages, the Ivatan seem to be of purer stock, a genetic makeup probably brought about by their isolation. They uniformly bear the features of their ancestors: the Malay's brown skin, the Chinese almond eyes and the Spaniard's aquiline nose.

The insularity of Batanes breeds special fears among the people. The Ivatan, according to anthropologist Dr. Florentino Hornedo, himself a native of Sabtang, are profoundly perturbed whenever a fellow Ivatan leaves the island. When Dr. Hornedo first left Sabtang for Manila to study, his neighbors came by with parting gifts—dried fish, yam, coconut, braids of garlic, chicken and other produce—which they handed him saying, "*Kawakayan mo ava yamen a manda d'kadmiman.* (Don't forget us until death)." He has come and gone many times since then, but he still gets the same sendoff every time he leaves Sabtang.

Writes Dr. Hornedo: "In this close-knit, faraway community, departures carry a sense of finality. That someone who steps off the island may never come back is a grim possibility. If the typhoon doesn't get him, the lure of a better life elsewhere will. Many of those who left in the old days for *pangavangan*, our term for Luzon and beyond, have not been heard from again. Those left behind console themselves by remembering these 'lost' relatives 'until death.'"

STRIKE UP a conversation with any Ivatan and eventually you'll be talking about the weather. The *añin*, or typhoon, is the central fact of Ivatan life and the source of stories, which in the retelling, take on mythic proportions. We heard several during our stay: In 1921 the cathedral's roof was blown off and the wireless tower twisted; in 1918, a fishing boat was swept away to Annam; in 1984, a fisherman was set adrift and wound up in Taiwan; in 1952 someone determined to recover his G.I. tin roof chased after it and found it in the town plaza rolled into a perfectly round ball; in 1987 a Philippine Navy LST ran aground in Basco and the school building in Mahatao was blown down. Mahatao now has a new school to replace the old one whose debris was never found, the Navy boat is beached at Basco's pier, a realistic prop for children's war games. Governor Castillejo's own story was of a stormy night when he was a child, when the family gathered in the kitchen waiting for the typhoon to pass. Suddenly the roof caved in, dropping a full-grown cow at their feet. The next day, there was a feast at the Castillejo's house.

THE TYPICAL Ivatan house is a fortress made of limestone and *cogon* grass designed to withstand winds of up to 200 mph. The walls and roof are a meter thick; windows and doors are small and narrow. During a typhoon the entire house is placed under a rope net fastened to the ground with steel stakes.

The kitchen, a separate building, often bigger than the main house, is the most important part of the house. Built around a great stove, it is akin to a tribal campfire—warm, safe, a source of communal well-being. There is room for everyone, including the farm animals, so that on stormy nights, the kitchen resembles Noah's ark.

Having lived with the typhoon, the Ivatan can tell when one is on its way. When the *aruyo* trees grow unusually long, tender leaves, it is time to fill the kitchen with provisions. Rice and yam are stored in baskets, fish is smoked and strung above the stove and drinking water is collected in earthen jars.

On sunny days the kitchen serves as a workroom for sundry chores such as carpentry or mending fishing nets.

ON OUR last day in Batanes we wanted to go to Sabtang. The crossing by itself is high adventure. Due to strong currents and rough breakers, docking boats must be assisted by an onshore rope-and-pulley system, hand-cranked by eight able-bodied men. But we were undeterred since we heard that Sabtang was filled with curiosities, including hillside homes that hang out over the sea, allowing the fishermen to "work at home."

We also wanted to visit a valley in Sinacan where a scenic cemetery is guarded by a Nagwat Rock teetering atop a precipitous slope, and Savidug where there are prehistoric natural fortresses called *idyang*. In the old days, the villagers took refuge here during tribal wars. They built makeshift huts fenced by megalithic stone pillars still found in the area.

Bright and early we were at Ivana, on the beach in front of the church, to board the motorboat for Sabtang. We waited and waited and waited. No boat, and we could see why. We left Basco at 6:30 a.m. under a clear sky, but when we arrived at

Ivana clouds started drifting in, first in stray wisps and then in great masses as the minutes ticked by. The Balintang Channel, which separates Ivana from Sabtang, progressively changed color from green to almost black; and the wind, reasonably balmy earlier, kicked up, blowing cold and gusty. That's it for Sabtang, we agreed. Even if the boat came we wouldn't dare cross over in that weather.

Instead, we left the beach and headed for the hills. Eerie thoughts were still playing out in our minds as we reached the high meadows. They reminded us of English moors. Was it the wind or did we hear the ghostly voice of a woman calling out a name? "Heathcliff ..."

Racing against impending rain, young boys, none named Heathcliff, were breathlessly chasing their cattle uphill. We asked them why they were herding the animals away from the valley where we thought they would be safer from bad weather. They pointed to massive stone mausoleum-like structures, "barns," they said. The Ivatan, we learned later, had built weather-proof barns in the fields so farmers and their animals could immediately seek shelter in a sudden storm.

We followed the boys to the barn and stayed with them until the strong rain passed. When the sun shone again, we all rushed outdoors, thankful for the radiant sunlight and the robust scent of wet earth.

The weather held until the following day, and we flew back to Manila without incident.

Wedding bells in Basco

We were back in Basco in 1989. This time Sabtang was our priority, and if we gathered enough nerve, we might even take in Itbayat. Pag-asa, the weather station in Manila, assured us there was a window of fine weather and the forecast good for a week.

So why did things start on the wrong foot? Midway between Manila and Laoag (where the flight to Batanes made a stop-over), the pilot had an announcement no one who flies regurlarly (or even irregularly) ever wants to hear: "Due to mechanical problems we are turning around." A flashing indicator on the control panel said there was something wrong with the Sunriser's landing gear. We held our breath during the torturous 20-minute flight back to Manila, but at no point did our lives flash before our eyes. The only thing flashing on the plane was that stupid switch. It turned out the landing gear was fine, it was nothing but a computer glitch.

So, we loaded up again and tried once more for Batanes, this time making it. But that wasn't the end of our troubles. The moment we got settled at Mama Lily's in Basco, the skies opened up and dumped buckets on us. You can talk of fickle weather or say something a bit stronger about Pag-asa. With two disasters under our belt and the trip not even started yet, we felt like the Al Capp cartoon character, Joe Bltzplk, who forever wore a thunderstorm for a hat.

There went Sabtang for the second time. Two years ago we didn't make it, either, because of a storm. That time we hiked the highlands of Ivana, this time we spent the rest of the day hiking around Batan, going as far as Vulugan, an incredible beach entirely covered with stones that the lapping waves have flattened and polished over the centuries.

We also did some shopping, not in a store but in the streets. We begged an old lady to sell us her *vacol*, the Ivatan grass raincoat that resembles a Tina Turner wig. Figuring its musical association, it now hangs above our piano.

It was raining again the next day. "Cheer up," the governor said, "all is not lost." He told us to change to more decent clothes. We were going to a wedding.

Life is hard in Batanes, yet surprisingly some Ivatan stay on by choice. The governor's wife, an outsider, fell in love with Batanes at first sight and made it her home. Allowed a second life, Gregorio Delatao, 88, who has traveled far and wide in his youth, will live it again in Batanes, the best place he knows. Even those who have left the island for a more comfortable and perhaps more eventful life in Manila return on occasions to observe rituals and touch base with the only piece of earth they could call home. One such is Juliet Ponce, now a Manilan, who had flown back to Batanes after eight years of absence, to wed.

The wedding rite was pretty much the same as far as wedding ceremonies go, but the reception was something else. It was held in a vacant lot beside an old government building. Despite the weather, the whole wedding party and everybody else walked over. The only exception was the bride and groom who rode the governor's car. On the cleared lot stood a makeshift hall trimmed with coconut fronds, crepe paper and balloons. Colorful mats covered the dirt floor, a dense pile of *cogon* served as a roof. A *rondalla* orchestra was already playing when the groom and bride stood at the entrance. Coaxed by the celebrators (the entire population of Batan it seemed; since there were no formal invitations, anyone who cared to come was welcome) still standing outside in the rain, the newlyweds waltzed their way to a pair of throne-like chairs where they were seated to receive their guests. Now it was the guests' turn to enter the hall in what we supposed was Basco's pecking order: first the parents of the bride and groom, then the wedding sponsors, followed by the bridesmaids and the ushers and so on. Guests must dance too, and it didn't matter if they did it in pairs or by themselves. What mattered was tradition. After dancing, every dancer must pin money on the bride and groom to attract a life of prosperity. This went on for an hour or so, and when it was over, the wedded couple, looking like a peso haystack, had enough money on them to open a hefty bank account.

Dinner was served next door in the government building. The food was ferried in (cooking was done by neighbors in their own kitchens) by the basinful. In all, three cows, a dozen pigs, and who knows how many chickens were slaughtered for the feast. This was apart from mountains of the usual Batanes staples of violet yams, fish and crabs.

It was still pouring outside, a dreary day to warm an Englishman's heart. But we soon fell into the spirit of the celebration and after a while neither broken airplanes nor canceled boat rides could diminish the love and companionship we felt from and for these people.

On our third day, the weather report confirmed that a typhoon was brewing in the north. The thought of being stranded here made us edgy, mainly because we had deadlines to meet in Manila. "Any day the plane comes, you should go," advised the governor.

The plane generally comes in at around 8 a.m. and departs an hour later. By 7:30 our bags were packed and we loitered on the porch with ears keened to the sound of a jet engine flying by. No luck. We went through the same motions every day for the rest of the week. On our seventh day—ah, that magical number—the weather broke, the plane came and we left.

DID WE leave a little piece of our heart in Basco? Nah. But every time we pass the *vacol* over the piano, our thoughts go back to Batanes. There are plans to urbanize the province. It now has its own radio station and the Philippine Tourism Authority is building a hostel in Basco.

The young Ivatan must be agog with excitement. But what about the old who dread change? They must be searching the heavens for a balm. In the old days, the Ivatan believed that when they die they become stars. On cloudless nights, the Ivatan's dark world is lit by hundreds of brilliant stars. Up there nothing will ever change. Up there is a cairn to folk memory.

Walking among the clouds

As the Cordilleras rise up from the Central Luzon plains with such suddenness and drama, you have to believe the Ifugao who say these mountains were created by a divine hand.

Long ago, according to legend, the Ifugao land was so flat the great hunter Kabigat couldn't hear the echo of his hunting dogs bark. To help him, Bongabong, the chief god, ordered a three-day rain to flood the region. As the waters flowed to the sea, the force of the current caused the flat ground to rise, forming the Gran Cordillera range. Even today, the Ifugao say, on a quiet night, you can hear Kabigat's dogs chasing their prey through the sheer ravines.

We began our trip to the roof of Luzon at sea level along Roxas Boulevard, where we joined our traveling companions for the next five days: Erica and Manfred, a couple from Germany; Edmund, a manufacturer from Belgium; and Jean Paul, a ski instructor from Switzerland.

We introduced ourselves in a babel of tongues—the Germans spoke only German; the Swiss spoke French and English but no German; we could cope in German and English but not in French. Only the Belgian and Jerry, our Filipino guide, spoke French, German and English, so they had all the languages covered.

At 6:00 a.m., like a mini-United Nations, we boarded a land cruiser and rolled northeast through Bulacan and Nueva Ecija to reach Nueva Vizcaya, our gateway to the Cordilleras.

After close to six hours of driving across the flat, unaccented highway of the Central Plains, our bus finally turned its hood skyward. We had reached the foot of the mountains. Traffic thinned as the cement road gave way to gravel which later became a dirt track not much wider than our vehicle. It would be days before our European friends saw anything they could identify as a road again.

BANAUE WAS our first destination. We were happy to arrive, albeit tired, hungry and cold. Fortunately, the Banaue Hotel had dinner ready and a blazing fire going in a six-foot fireplace. After living in Manila for almost five years, we had forgotten what cold feels like; up in the mountains at 4,000 feet, we quickly remembered. By the third day we were longing for some heat.

Our first mountain morning came early: we rose at dawn, gathering in the dining room to watch the mist swirl down the rice terraces, casting weird shadows on the mountain walls and wet green fields. From our vantage point, the rice fields looked like a vast checkerboard. There is a no-nonsense feeling about these structures, perfect rectangles carved out of the landscape, extending as far as the eye can see.

The rice terraces belong to the Ifugao and their culturally distinct mountain cousins—the Bontoc, Apayao, Kalinga and Tinguian. The pioneering American anthropologist H. Otley Beyer links the mountain-terrace people with a migrant population that moved out of the South China-Tonkin area, bringing with them the knowledge of copper and rice some 2,000 years ago. Carbon-14 dating of the terraces, carried out by the Western Michigan University in 1973, has borne out Beyer's theory.

The Ifugao occupy the Polis range in the Gran Cordillera Central. Although the building of rice terraces is also known in neighboring mountain areas, its main concentration is in Ifugao country. The major terrace complex, centered around the towns of Hapao, Banaue, Hungduan, and Mayoyao, form the most extensive system of mountain terracing found anywhere in the world.

The enormousness of the task can only be fathomed in numbers and comparisons. To build the terraces with crude hand tools, the Ifugao had first to reinforce the entire base of the mountain with walls of hard soil or rocks gathered from the distant river banks. The stone walls extend at least two meters beneath the ground. It is believed that the aggregate weight of the stones used to build the base of the rice terraces surpasses that of the stones used to build the pyramids of Egypt. Furthermore, it is said, if put end to end the terraces would encircle half the globe. It is not surprising that the Banaue Rice Terraces have been described as the "Eighth Wonder of the World."

Later on in the trip we would have an opportunity to hike down the terrace rim and meet some of the people whose ancestors had defied common sense and topography and built these rice fields in the sky.

BANGA-AN IS a tiny village set in a bowl of the mountain. Up on the ledge, where the land begins to dip into a valley, you can faintly hear the sounds of village life bouncing off the mountain walls: domestic animals, children, snatches of loud conversation. Only when you approach the rim and look down can you see the village below, with its brown huts huddled close together, floating like an island amid a sea of water-logged rice fields.

Squatting under his hut, Anton Hamboknon shyly responded to our questions. He doesn't know how old he is, but we guessed his age to be about 35. He has five children, livestock and a skeleton of a Japanese soldier which he would show us for P20.

Like many of his generation, Anton straddles two worlds. He answers to a Christian name, but his teeth are black from chewing betel nut. He is a self-taught carver, creating the ritual objects of his tribe while listening to a Kenny Rogers song on the radio. Anton is embarrassed when he is with strangers because he can't read and knows very little of the world beyond Banga-an. He is a man of the seasons—he knows when to plant, when to harvest and when to rest, telling time by the shape of the moon. His children, who attend the local school, live by the calendar and the clock. He knows, too, that like so many other village youths, his own will someday leave the terraces for jobs in Manila or even abroad.

Before we left Anton we bought an Ifugao harvest knife whose handle he had carved into the shape of a *bulol*, the traditional rice god. The Ifugao have 1,500 different gods. Into this deific wealth of the Cordilleras the western missionaries are still trying to bring them just one. We saw some missionaries, freshly scrubbed and full of idealism, in almost every town and village. Our Belgian companion met a nun from Antwerp who has lived in these mountains for more than 50 years. Is their proselytizing succeeding? Many of the villagers we encountered wore crucifixes, so maybe now the Ifugao have 1,501 gods.

We were reluctant to leave Banaue. It is like a hanging garden. Wild orchids, hibiscus, poinsettia and strawberry cling to the mountainsides, while the low lying edges of the land are carpeted with sunflowers, calla lilies and cottony cogon grass. "Can you imagine this?" asked Erica via the Belgian manufacturer. "In Germany lilies cost 30 marks apiece. Here you just find them on the road." Even the rice terraces below us sparkled with floral color. In the paddies, the Ifugao plant *dongla*, a tall shrub with long, dark red leaves, to mark property lines. But the plant also serves as a grave marker, since some Ifugao still bury their dead in the paddies. In the not too distant past, *dongla* decorated the warriors' headdresses, its bold red color signifying the wearer's ferocity.

FROM BANAUE we headed deeper into the mountains and farther north into Bontoc, also known as the Mountain Province. It is easy to tell when you have crossed the border. The Ifugao terraces are concave and generally have walls of mud; those in Bontoc are convex and use stone walls. The severe checkerboarding of the landscape also surrenders to terraces carved into fanciful shapes.

The Bontoc are richer than the Ifugao. Rather than depend solely on rice for their cash crop, they have a triennial harvest of vegetables and tubers. Perhaps this is why they seem to be more playful about their work.

The Bontoc village of Bayo-o is particularly charming. The vegetable fields of cabbage, carrots, potato, broccoli and lettuce are arranged into circles, mazes and arcs. Occasionally, a farmer took a stab at immortality and spelled out his initials. From afar, the stone walls of Bayo-o resemble the Great Wall of China and the vegetables a miniature topiary garden.

The towns in Bontoc offer two surprises. The first is structural. Although most of the houses here look like their counterparts everywhere else in the Philippines, they are made entirely of G.I. tin. We couldn't figure out why. Metal is a terrible insulator and we saw plenty of wood, including pine, an excellent building material. The best explanation Jerry, our guide, could come up with was "tradition," which in this case, left much to be desired. The other surprise is visual. Every house has a chimney. It doesn't sound like much, but when seen in the tropical Philippines, it certainly leaps out at you.

The tribal people of the Cordilleras are generally referred to as Igorot. In the capital town of Bontoc, a museum gathers and displays their cultural artifacts. Founded by Sister Basil Gekiere, ICM, and designed after the traditional Bontoc house, it contains a wide variety of objects: models of different types of tribal houses; precious Kalinga beads made of glass, porcelain, gold and stone; a carabao-toe container for roasted rice; brass gongs originally imported from China (many bearing human jawbone handles as proof that the owner had taken a head); the works of Edward Masferre and Kip Moore, two master photographers who have devoted their lives to recording Igorot lifestyles in the early 1900s; and a copy of the *Ethnographic Atlas of the Ifugao* by Harold Conklin, published by the American Geographical Society of New York and Yale University Press. There are even pictures of Bontoc's first American governor general, John Evans, a remarkable figure who resembles Jeremy Irons in *The French Lieutenant's Woman.*

IN MID-AFTERNOON we reached Sagada, a serene village dominated by the imposing, 100-year old St. Mary's Church. The Episcopal institution can be seen from almost any point in the town, so it must be visible from the *dap-uy*, the spiritual center of every Bontoc village that Christianity has been slowly relegating to nothing more than an icon of the past.

In tour books and brochures, Sagada is known as the town of the Bontoc animists, the hometown of Masferre and the adopted home of William Henry Scott, a scholar of Philippine prehistory and the Cordilleras. To others, however, Sagada is known for inexpensive but potent marijuana. The plant is said to be cultivated here in profusion and a tourist wandering around town is bound to encounter a hawker plying "good smokes." For better or for worse, depending upon your point of view, Sagada has become a haven for Europeans and Americans who have "dropped out" and are "searching for the meaning of life."

While sitting in a Sagada café, we met Romualdo Aben, a 77-year-old native, who as a boy had Masferre as a teacher in grade school. He was a delightful storyteller, although it quickly became apparent that while he knew a great deal about Sagada, its history and its people, he didn't know any hidden secrets of the universe, nor the "meaning of life."

If there is a secret in Sagada, it is how they mummified the corpses found in the burial caves above the town. We were told they used guava leaves and saltwater to protect the corpse from time and the elements. Unfortunately this solution couldn't protect the dead from vandals. Many of the coffins and their contents have been stolen.

We reached the Mount Data Hotel before dark. Nestled in a foggy pine forest and built around a great fireplace, the hotel made our Swiss companion homesick. It had the feeling of a ski lodge in his native land, he said. All that was missing to complete the illusion were people with broken legs. Erica and Manfred, warming themselves by the fire, had their own view of things. "If we knew it would be this cold in the Philippines, we would have gone to Austria instead," they said.

The next day, before the fog had lifted, we were off for Benguet and its premier city, Baguio, which was a full eight-hour drive away. But first we stopped in Mount Timbac to have a look at the 500-year-old Kabayan mummies interred in the mountain caves.

The Ibaloi, the tribe to whom the mummies belong, couldn't have found a more ghostly place to keep their dead. On Mount Timbac you literally walk on the clouds. The wind sighs and the pines drip with Spanish moss so thick and colorless that from afar they seem like cobwebs spun by a species of giant spiders. Our local guide, Moses, himself an Ibaloi, regaled us with stories as he took our group some 300 steps down the mountainside. "Sometimes the mummies shun visitors," he told us. "Roy, our driver, at one time tried to take a picture of the mummies with four different cameras and nothing came out."

ONCE WE passed the highest point of the Philippine highway system (7,400 feet), we began traveling downhill. We had been so high for so long that when we finally reached Baguio, our next destination, it felt like the lowlands.

We hadn't been to Baguio for years. Seeing it now was like seeing a new place. The city has become too crowded, and to ease the flow of human traffic around the market area, the government has constructed pedestrian flyovers. The market, once an enchanting emporium of highland curiosities, now reeked with the commercialism of a department store.

New hotels crowd around Burnham Park, and Baguio drivers, who once had the reputation of being the most courteous in the Philippines, have picked up all the bad habits of their Manila cousins. Some of the old landmarks are still there—Rosebowl, the popular Chinese restaurant; Patria Hotel, favored by students; the Cathedral with its majestic spires; and the Session Theater, now a bit ragged at the edges but spiritedly fending off demolition. But too much has been demolished, including a lot of Baguio's charm.

Still, we were delighted to be in Baguio, if only because we could sit down again to a decent meal. We were finally off the "*pancit* express." On the road in Ifugao and Bontoc, our lunches never exceeded the gustatory heights of sauteed Chinese noodles. It was worse in the hinterlands of Benguet, where the specialty of roadside stalls was mystery meat, which, for lack of a more palatable description, was how we translated the scribbling on the menu for our European friends. How else were we to explain that the dishes listed down referred to choice parts of a dog cooked in ways inscrutable to the Western imagination? When *pancit* wasn't available, we settled for overripe bananas.

After our long, unvarying intake of pancit and stale fruits, we dined with relief—and greed—at Baguio's Club John Hay, stuffing ourselves with thick steak sandwiches and bowls of chocolate ice cream.

WE EXPECTED this trip to be an experience of the past, and it was. But it was also a foretaste of the future. This feeling was never more intense than in Banaue. Unless the young return to the heartland to carry on their ancestors' agricultural tradition, the rice terraces will be gone in a matter of decades, completely reclaimed by vegetation. We saw too many instances of it happening already.

The thought also came to us while looking at a Masferre classic photograph from the '50s of a Bontoc elder wearing a Yale lock in his ear instead of the traditional earring. Today's Igorot has lost much more than an earring—they have swapped their tribal names for Christian ones; they wear jeans instead of G-strings, baseball caps instead of basket hats; they have traded their love of the land for an allegiance to the paycheck.

Lovely as the Cordilleras are, what we saw was a diminished version of its former beauty. And now the question is how long these mountains can hold out before they become a diminished version of a diminished version.

All quiet on the apparition front

American journalist Horace Greeley said, "Go west!" The Department of Tourism has been saying, "Go south." So naturally, we decided to go north to explore an area that since 1993 has been largely forgotten: Agoo.

Not that Agoo is a town where nothing happens. In the last 10 years Agoo has been the scene of a double calamity and a miracle. The calamities drew the nation's sympathy; the miracle brought the nation to its knees.

On July 16, 1990, the ground shook. The same earthquake that devastated Baguio also wreaked havoc on Agoo. A lesser people would have broken down or been reduced to inaction by despair. But not the Ilocanos, who for centuries mocked nature's ill will with their own will to exist. As soon as the aftershocks were over, the folk of Agoo began rebuilding the town.

But no matter how many resources man can employ, when nature is in an impish mood she always seems to have another trick up her sleeve. Just a year later, all the painstaking reconstruction was swept away when typhoon "Trining" blasted through Ilocandia taking much of Agoo with it. The town had to be rebuilt once again.

Today, as you walk the broad, leafy streets of Agoo, the effects of the double disaster are still evident, even though the rubble has been cleaned up. A bell tower that used to stand over there doesn't, the *Santo Niño de Pescador* Wayside Shrine now exists only in guidebooks. And the Marcos Resthouse, described as the Malacañang of the North, lies in ruins, its in-ground swimming pool sitting a meter above ground while the once opulent living room of the main house now houses only bats.

A YOUNG boy standing on a hill in Agoo saw a vision. The Virgin Mary appeared—again. Agoo has been the site of more than 270 reported apparitions and miracles since the 1900s and The Miraculous Spring (Mary's Well) has been an Adoration site since the 1970s. So for the elders, while this latest manifestation was wonderful, there was no cause for hysteria. The locals dutifully went to Apparition Hill to pray, expecting the Virgin Mary to let them know what she wanted in her own time.

But somehow, this appearance made it into the national newspapers and for about three months in 1993 Agoo became the focus of a global pilgrimage. Every day more than 80,000 people climbed the steep ramps of Apparition Hill and later came down to speak of miraculous experiences—a dancing sun, mysterious lights that came from nowhere like laser beams, sweet aromas, and base metal rosary beads turning to gold. Others, perhaps less religiously inclined, talked of UFO sightings. Some even presented "evidence" such as a Polaroid picture of a spectral Christ taken by a *balikbayan*. It was a wild and eerie time in Agoo. Then as suddenly as it all started, it stopped.

Today all is quiet on the apparition front. The hill has reverted back to nature. There are some volunteers who attend to the occasional pilgrims who still show up, usually on Saturday when Judiel Nieva, the boy who started it all, leads a procession. Venders, as always, ever-expectant, half-heartedly keep their lean-to shops stocked with religious images and empty bottles to be filled with the water from St. Mary's Well. And bored children break off their games and rush to the infrequent tricycle to sell its passengers candles and prayer sheets. It's all reminiscent of a gold-rush town after the mines have been tapped out.

THE ENTIRE region surrounding Agoo is deeply religious. Whether you approach the town from the north or the south along the National Highway, the road is bordered on both sides with beautiful old churches. "You have to be religious if you're Ilocano," says a native son. "You need a lot of soul to love Ilocos, which lies between a rock and a hard place."

Upon entering Agoo the first thing that catches the eye is the Basilica, the only one north of Manila, dedicated to Our Lady of Charity. The Basilica achieved some dubious fame in recent years for its painting of The Second Coming of Christ, in which Imelda Marcos has been depicted as an angel.

The original church, founded in 1578, was destroyed by an earthquake in 1872. The second church, where the long venerated *Virgen de la Caridad* was canonically crowned, was demolished in 1975 for a new Marian shrine consecrated in December 1978. It was elevated to the rank of Basilica Minore by Pope John Paul II in 1982. As proof of Ilocano craftsmanship, the present structure shows virtually no signs of the extensive reconstruction work done after the earthquake of 1990.

In addition to its importance in the religious life of Agoo, the church is also a treasure trove of local and European art. Of special note are the two wooden bas reliefs near the altar which tell the story of Agoo's founding. One panel depicts the arrival of the first Franciscan missionaries in 1578. The other panel narrates the story of Agoo's first miracle—Father Sebastian de Baeza, one of the two founding fathers of Agoo, restoring life to a dead child.

For some reason, most of the guidebooks focus on the Basilica's architecture, yet miss its organ, the largest working pipe organ in the Philippines. (The organ in the Manila Cathedral is larger, but one of the manuals doesn't play). Built and installed by Peter Wegenbach of West Germany, the Basilica's organ has three manuals and a pedal board controlling 2,800 pipes, including a rank of Spanish trumpets. On the first Sunday of each month, under the musical direction of Florent Sals, the Basilica's 40-voice mixed choir performs a program of Latin motets, Gregorian chants and plainsongs in celebration of High Mass.

Professor Sals came to the Philippines from Belgium in 1948. A music student and later a music teacher in Antwerp, he has been music director for the Basilica since its dedication. His wife Lila, an accomplished keyboard player, is the Basilica's organist.

While we were there we heard a program of Palestrina, Buencamino and the *Missa Brevis* by Von de Steen, as well as a medley of Ilocano folk songs such as *Pamulinawen*. "Have you ever performed Gounod's *Saint Cecilia's Mass*?" we asked, a piece which we felt would be ideal for an organ and choir that size. "Send us the score and we will," Sals replied. "I am always looking for new pieces to expand the repertoire, but full scores are hard to find in the Philippines." Fortunately, we had the orchestral score of the Gounod work, so we copied it and sent it up. Unfortunately, we were on the road elsewhere when Sals premiered excerpts of the *Mass*.

NOT FAR from the Basilica, about 15 minutes north on the National Highway, is the fishing village of Santa Rita. Although it is best known as the location of the Marcos Resthouse, it is also the site of a beautiful white chapel, *Santa Rita de Cascia*.

The chapel, which is brand-new, comes with a story. An earlier chapel built on the same site faced the road. Not too long after it was completed, the structure collapsed for no apparent reason, leading the folk to believe it was destroyed by the Virgin Mary, who wanted her chapel to face the sea. This chapel not only faces the sea, but the Virgin's image is on the beach. Inside, the image of the Sto. Niño is standing in a banca dressed as a fisherman, holding a net, an oar and a fish.

Although we saw some sea-going bancas with their fine white nylon nets, it seems the popular fishing method in Sta. Rita is the drag net. One end of a large heavy net is attached to a small banca, the other end is controlled by five or six people on the beach. The banca goes out, turns around and starts coming into shore, creating a mobile fish pond. The trapped fish are then shared by everyone who helped land them. The ritual is repeated over and over, from first light in the morning until midday.

THE POPULAR home industries in La Union are pottery and weaving. The potters are located on both sides of the highway between San Fernando and Agoo. The open-air stalls offer a vast collection—flower pots in every size and shape, cooking pots, decorative pots, pots whose use we could only guess at, all made on site and decorated by hand.

The weaving cooperatives are in Bangar, a three-hour drive from Agoo through La Union's tobacco fields. Although the fields had already been harvested, we could still see the drying towers, looking like medieval castles dotting the brown earth.

Weaving factories here can be one loom in a private home or several looms in a garage-like structure. Stepping into a weaving shed was stepping back centuries. In the shed we visited, two women were sitting at one large loom passing the shuttle back and forth across the expanse of strings. At another loom there sat an ancient woman of indeterminate age smoking a fat black cigar. With fixed concentration, her gnarled tobacco-stained fingers moved around the warp with the agility of a teenager playing the piano as she created the patterns that the two younger women would weave.

The pattern is formed by tying hundreds of knots in the warp thread. It is a skill passed down from mother to daughter and takes decades to master. Each pattern needs a different arrangement of knots and there can be dozens of patterns in a finished piece. Today the women were weaving a blanket for a single bed. As we watched the three women labor in semidarkness, we wondered if Bangar had ever heard of the power loom.

Returning to Agoo we made a slight detour to Naguilian in search of a different cottage industry. Naguilian is famous throughout La Union as the best place to buy *basi*, the Ilocano wine. Made by boiling sugarcane juice with *duhat* bark and guava leaves, it tastes like a cross between altar wine and Jewish *kosher* wine. History tells us that *basi* is a drink that Ilocanos will die for. In 1807 they mounted a revolt when the Spaniards imposed a wine monopoly which prevented the Ilocano farmers from making their favorite brew. Actually, the farmers had something to be riled about. *Basi* is wonderful stuff and we brought back several gallons of the purple brew for ourselves and friends in Manila.

ON OUR last day we went to the Ilokos Museum, a replica of the northern all-weather house. The guidebooks say it will "display the arts and crafts of the Ilocandia." Perhaps it will but it didn't yet. All we saw was a guard's change of shirt displayed on a wire hanger. The rest of the museum building was empty. So we suppose when we come back this will be our first stop.

The next time around we will also be more methodical shoppers. The La Union region is a bargain hunter's paradise. You just have to know what to buy and where to go: *bagoong* in Agoo; mangoes and bamboo-craft in Caba; pottery in San Juan; *abel Iloco* in Bangar and last but never least, *basi* in Naguilian.

Do the loop

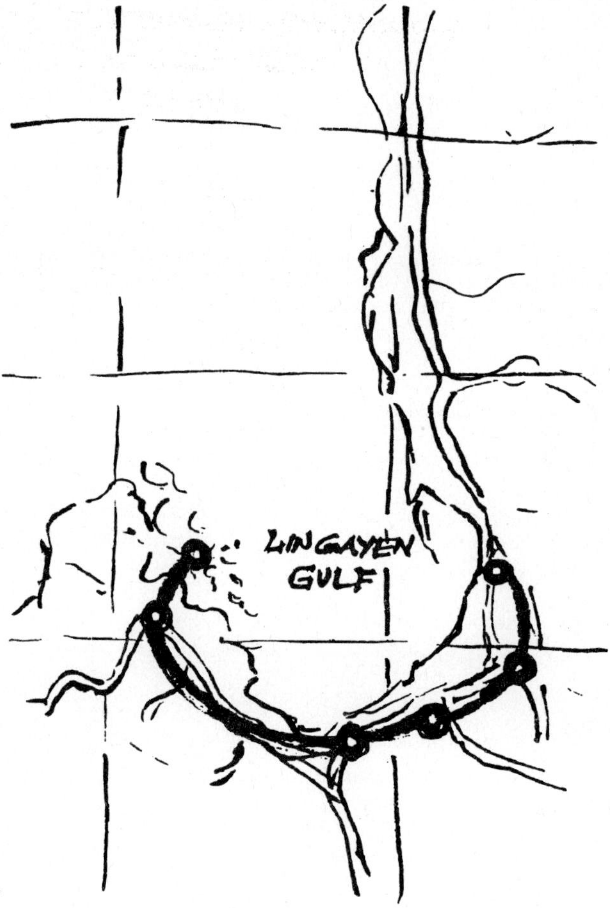

If you look at the Philippine map and draw a line connecting Manila, Tarlac, Urdaneta, San Fabian, Dagupan, Lingayen, Lucap and back to Manila via Bugallon, you'll form a loop, something resembling a cowboy's lasso. This was our route for a three-day trip.

Like so many others, we've often passed through Pangasinan en route to Baguio or Vigan, but we haven't really done the province justice. It's really our loss. Pangasinan deserves much more than just a passing glance from a bus window.

You know you're in Pangasinan when the chain of rice fields from Bulacan to Tarlac is broken by fishponds, mangroves, saltbeds and estuaries rimmed by oyster farms. Now, in addition to carabaos, you also see a waterworld: *salambaw* fishing boats resting like fragile conversation pieces and the radiant sky mirrored in a vast reflecting pool.

All Pangasinan towns are never too far away from water. Three river systems, including the great Agno River, which originates from the Grand Central Cordillera, flow into the province's plains and deltas. Annually, during the typhoon season, these inland waters swell, claiming lives and produce, but also spawning crustaceans and freshwater fish while irrigating the rice, tobacco and sugarcane fields.

In the west, the province's bounty extends beyond the water's edge. Facing the South China Sea, the coastline curves inward at the Gulf of Lingayen, then spreads outward again at Cape Bolinao giving rise to a fishing industry as ancient as the sea itself. Pangasinan *bangus*, especially the Dagupan variety, are famous even in an archipelago not lacking for this fish.

The thriving fishing industry had spun off another livelihood resource that gave the province its name: the manufacture of salt by water evaporation. Pangasinan means the place where *asin*, the native word for "salt," is made.

ALL OF this, just a stone's throw from Manila, was there for us if we would just slow down and see it. So, one fine summer day, in a motoring mood, we decided to "do the loop." Our starting point would be San Fabian.

San Fabian by the sea is an excellent place to stretch out after that three-hour ride from Manila. The beach is inviting: smooth, rock-free and safe, as the water stays only waist-deep up to about a hundred meters from shore.

A number of resorts dot the seaside barrio of Bolasi, including the San Fabian Beach Resort where we spent the night. Our choice motivated as much by curiosity as by economics. The resort once belonged to the Marcoses, and we wouldn't pass up the chance to take a peep at the bullet-proof presidential suite that allegedly has a "toilet with a silencer." Bulletproofing is easy enough to imagine, but a silent toilet?

Well, there it was. As expected, the bedroom walls were thick and, unless shot at by a high-powered weapon, impregnable. A veritable bunker whose invincibility was concealed from the common eye by, of all things, department store Filipiniana decor. Was this a joke on the would-be assassin and on the victim? As to the noiseless flush, it functioned true to its claim, sucking in everything with astonishing discretion. We were impressed but we never found out if the past owners were likewise awed since the Marcoses visited San Fabian just three times and stayed only a few hours on each occasion. Today the facility is open to the public and anyone can rent the Marcos bunker if it's available.

The resort is situated on the edge of the beach and there is a marker at the water's edge which cites three historic landings (we supposed in order of importance): General Douglas MacArthur, on January 9, 1945, to liberate Northern Luzon from the Japanese; General Lloyd Wheaton, on November 7, 1899, at the height of the Filipino-American War, to intercept the forces of General Emilio Aguinaldo; and General Masaharu Homma leading the Kamaya and Tanaka Brigade of the Japanese Army, on December 22, 1941. Like Leyte, Pangasinan is steeped in WW II history.

San Fabian is also a good jumping-off place for excursions to nearby towns like Dagupan and Manaoag, which are just a 20-minute drive away.

In Dagupan City, the attraction is the Dagupan Poolside and Seafood Restaurant. Practically brand-new, the facility was built as a venue for *Palarong Pambansa* swimming competitions. Adults pay P60 and children P40 to use the Olympic-size swimming pool, an equally huge wading pool and shower stalls equipped with lockers.

A couple of laps in the pool worked up our appetite for guiltless gorging at the poolside restaurant. The activity started in the restaurant's "market" where we picked out our food from an overwhelming array of fresh seafoods, vegetables and fruits. The kitchen cooked it just the way we wanted it while we waited to be served in the adjoining dining room. The shrimp *kinilaw* was heavenly, sweet and spicy all at once; the *sinigang na malaga* melted in our mouth; broiled Dagupan *bangus*, a must, and the pork chops were cooked to a turn. Boiled eggplant, okra, green mangoes and tomatoes were paired off with *bagoong isda*, Pangasinan's signature dipping sauce. All this was served with steaming, fragrant rice. We ended our meal with ripe mangoes and watermelon. The best part was, this delectable feast costs only about P150 per person, or about the price of a meal of "dead" food in a Manila fast food joint.

MANAOAG SERVES up a different kind of nourishment. People come here to worship at the shrine of the Lady of the Holy Rosary, popularly known as *Nuestra Señora de Manaoag* or simply *Apu Baket*. We regretted missing the miraculous lady's procession by a few days. In a week's time she would be dressed in her finery, ensconced on a silver *carroza* and taken to the streets, her way paved by some 20,000 votive candles.

Manaoag used to be called Santa Monica, after the patron saint of the first Christian mission established here by the Augustinians in 1595. How it became Manaoag is recounted in a folk story. A farmer on his way home from the fields was surprised by a glowing tree that took the form of the Virgin Mary. "Build my church on this spot," the Lady told him. Astounded, the farmer raced to the mission house to deliver the Lady's message, but the priest dismissed the incident as merely a native's fantasy brought on by summer heat. However, the farmer's story spread throughout the region and soon folk from neighboring communities started pouring into town. When asked where they came from, pilgrims would say, "*Dinad Apo ya mantatawag*" ("from the Lady who calls"). The phrase was eventually shortened to Manaoag.

Folktales also describe a nipa chapel that was built on the spot where the Virgin appeared. But to give her a more fitting home, a large wooden church was erected beside the original Chapel of Santa Monica in Baloquin. On the morning that the image of the Lady was to be brought to her new home, some people rushed in nervously shouting that the church had disappeared. Everyone rushed to the site. There was no trace of the structure, not even a scrap of wood. Thus a brick church was built where the nipa chapel stood.

The present church, constructed in 1901, retains many of the features of the old brick church which was destroyed by an earthquake in 1892. The main altar is laid out under a colossal, octagonal dome painted with the 15 Mysteries of the Rosary. Behind the altar is the *retablo* holding the life-size ivory image of the Virgin of Manaoag that Fr. Juan de San Jacinto, the Dominican who took over the Augustinian mission in 1600, brought from Spain. In the Adoration Chapel, at the back of the church, pilgrims can touch the Virgin's dress and drop in letters of petition. The chapel also contains religious statuary and the gold cape the Virgin wore at the 50th anniversary of her coronation.

Always richly dressed, the Virgin of Manaoag has a fabulous and extensive wardrobe. "They're gifts from devotees," explains *sacristan mayor*, Jaime Soriano, who dresses the statue and maintains the church's fleet of *carrozas*. "Each of her many gowns is worth over a hundred thousand pesos, and since the Virgin changes clothes only four times a year, there's enough in the collection to last ten years."

OUR NEXT stop on the loop was Lingayen. Architecturally—and in many ways also culturally—Pangasinan's capital town has two distinct areas. Inland, the older district, built in the Spanish style, contains the population center clustered around the church. Closer to the Gulf, the other district, called the Government Center, harks back to the American colonial regime. The area is reminiscent of Washington, D.C., if on a modest scale. Graced by wide-crowned flame trees, its main road leads to the central capitol building, an edifice of marble columns, wide stairways and intricate iron-work. A scowling eagle, a veritable piece of Americana, is perched on the banister of a beautiful spiral staircase.

It was built as part of American reparations after the war. The American liberation forces under the command of General Walter Krueger landed in the Lingayen-Dagupan-Mabilao area on the morning of January 9, 1945. The event, although victorious and welcome, was disastrous for the local population. Believing that the Japanese would open fire from foxholes on the beach as they did in Leyte, the American troops strafed Lingayen before coming ashore. Unfortunately, the Japanese had already re-treated and instead hundreds of Filipino civilians were killed while the shelling reduced the original government complex to rubble.

"The best view is from up there," said our guide from the Lingayen Gulf Hotel, pointing to the capitol's rooftop. We climbed up for a panoramic view of Lingayen Gulf. At this time of the day it was glittering tinsel. This is a perfect setting for a party, we remarked, imagining what the place would look like in the evening, under the moon, stars and strings of party lights winking in rhythm with the lamps of the fishing boats out in the Gulf.

It was too late to patent our idea. The patrician Philippine President Manuel L. Quezon beat us to it some sixty years earlier, holding elegant receptions on the building's roof. And in more recent times, the government used the roof for a gala party celebrating the commemoration of the 50th Anniversary of the Lingayen Gulf Landings.

In front of the capitol is an outdoor war memorial containing some of the hardware left behind—a Japanese Zero Fighter, American anti-aircraft guns and two Sherman tanks. Kids play wargames around them now, unaware of their once lethal power.

Flanking the memorial are two other new buildings, neither of which quite blends with the dated capitol building and war memorial. One resembles a Disneyland reproduction of a Thai grand house, complete with an ornate triangular roof trimmed at the edges with upswept eaves. The structure, we learned, is the governor's residence and office. We wanted to find out if the building was as fancy inside and possibly get to meet the governor as well. However, we were twice disappointed. The governor was in Manila, and the building's interiors were characteristically government-issued.

The other building, the Sison Auditorium, is modeled along the lines of Art Nouveau. It was built in time for the Landing Anniversary and *Palarong Pambansa* but now stands like a pricey (its sophisticated sound system alone must have cost millions) paperweight until the government decides what to do with it.

LESS THAN an hour's drive from Lingayen is the town of Alaminos, famous for the Hundred Islands. Scattered off the coast of barrio Lucap, these dome-shaped islands, 123 of them, many still unnamed, dot the Lingayen Gulf. A strong swimmer can swim from island to island. We island-hopped on a boat.

If the choice were ours, we would have headed for the sequestered islands, but our *bangkero*, used to ferrying popular tourists, took us to Quezon Island, a "must-see," he said. The most overwhelming sight here was that of a beach packed with people—so many black heads bobbing on the green waters, so many brown bodies toasting on the white sand. Why it was filled was understandable. It costs practically nothing—just boat fare—to come here, if you bring your own food. And the best bargain is the lovely, leafy beach and clear sea.

Still, not in the mood to jump in with the madding crowd, we strolled around the island. Interestingly, it is also the principal laboratory of Count 100, short for Conserve Our Unique National Treasures. Now on its second year, the movement was launched by several government agencies, including the PTA (Philippine Tourism Autority) and the University of the Philippines Marine Science Institute (UPMSI), to re-seed marine life in Hundred Islands National Park. An extensive undersea breeding project, Quezon Island's waters are being restocked with artificial reefs and giant clams.

Our walk ended at the toes of Manuel Quezon's boots. Up on a hill stands the monument of the Philippine president after whom the island was named. He is presented here at his regal best—in his favorite riding breeches. A bit further downhill are a pair of huge, pink, plaster swans looking out on the sea. We weren't able to confirm the accuracy of our calculations, but we figured if we were out there on the sea, across from where we were now standing, and we looked back in this direction, we would see a rather imperious Mr. Quezon, in full riding regalia, astride two candy-colored swans.

HUNDRED ISLANDS closed the loop. From there we drove back to Manila through the scenic gulf towns of Alaminos and Sual, then the inland towns of Bugallon, Aguilar and Magtaren which connect to Tarlac, an equally interesting province waiting to be discovered.

A gathering of artists

"Art is life," says Alfonso "Coke" Bolipata, taking the adage "art imitates life" one step further. Explains he: "It's wrong to segregate away the beautiful, bringing it out only in select venues and at appointed times. Art isn't an occasion, it's a part of the regimen of living."

Coke, an internationally renowned violinist, has been living in an artistic milieu since he was born. His grandfather, Ramon Corpus, was also a violinist; an aunt, Anita Magsaysay-Ho, is a recognized name in Philippine painting; his parents once published a literary magazine; and his brothers, cellist Ramon and pianist Jaime, were both child prodigies and are now world-class musicians. "As a child I remember that table conversation could revolve around anything, from someone's new interpretation of a Mozart concerto to the latest short story by Greg Brillantes, a frequent visitor at our home." For a young boy it was an environment which took the arts out of the museum, library and concert hall and implanted them into the most mundane parts of daily routine.

In 1993, at age 29, Coke initiated a bold plan that would recreate the world he grew up in for the rest of the artistic community in the Philippines. "I wanted to build a refuge where artists could gather, work, discuss and experiment. A place that would also, coincidentally, break down the artificial walls between their disciplines and nurture collaborations and appreciation of each other's art forms. I am reminded of the parable of the three blind men and the elephant. One 'sees' a wall, another a snake, the third a tree. Had they compared notes they would have realized they were all looking at the same thing. In the 'cultural Eden' I envisioned, artists could take the time to compare notes."

Beginning in October 1993, with the aid of his family and a dedicated coterie of volunteers, the Casa San Miguel Center for the Arts broke ground at the Corpus family summer estate in San Antonio, Zambales. Five months later, it opened its doors. The art colony is lodged in a mango orchard close to the sea and surrounded by the Pundaquit Mountains. The ideal environment offers both the inspiration and isolation needed for creative work.

The Art Center looks like a large farmhouse, blending into its rural surroundings. Any resemblance to a farmhouse, however, stops at the facade. The interior reminds one of a *Klein Bottle*, the mathematician Christian Klein's theoretical three-dimensional object rotated into the fourth dimension. Rooms open onto rooms with a dizzying irregularity. The placement of windows and skylights make it almost impossible to judge inside and outside walls. And to top it off, literally, there is an octagonal cupola with an unobstructed 360-degree view of the countryside.

A work-dedicated building, the Center has a 350-seat air-conditioned concert hall, a two-story art gallery, a great hall for large installations, practice areas, dormitories for resident artists and two art libraries. Outside there is a 600-seat amphitheater.

"IF YOU build it, they will come," said potter Jaime de Guzman, quoting the now-famous line from *Field of Dreams*, as he sized up Casa San Miguel. Indeed, as soon as the structure was built, it was filled with creators, creations, appreciators and the curious. On one weekend in February we found writers Gilda Cordero-Fernando, Mariel Francisco, Fe Arriola, Nestor Mata and Odette Alcantara; visual artists Roberto Feleo, Brenda Fajardo, Jaime de Guzman, Ann Wizer, BenCab and Alan Cosio; dancers Denisa Reyes and Myra Beltran; soprano Mariana Ivanova, pianist Cecile Roxas and music critic Pablo Tariman all visiting or working at the Center. Best of all, for Coke, the Center was drawing in the Zambal *aetas*, as well as the folk of San Antonio and the surrounding Zambales towns.

Says Coke: "Art originated with the people, as a means of interpreting the world and organizing their environment; 'high art' merely moved it to a more sophisticated plane, but in no way abandoned its primary roots. Therefore art in any form, as an acknowledgment of its progenitor, should be accessible to everyone. As an artist, I thought, I didn't have to be in a tuxedo to be creative. And while we can't extend what we are doing to the entire country, by being here in a small rural community, we can reach at least some of the common *tao*."

The concerts began and the folk came, clad in slippers and T-shirts, on foot or by tricycle. For most of them, it was a first brush with classical music. The response was tremendous. They wouldn't let go of a Lithuanian pianist, rousing him to play encore after encore. At another concert, Haydn's *Black Saturday* quartet moved the audience to tears.

The Casa was on the right track.

STILL, CASA San Miguel couldn't live on good intentions alone. Like any other institution, it learned soon enough that it needed outside funding to achieve its objectives. Finally reorganized as a foundation, Casa San Miguel could apply for grants. Their Sec-

and Pundaquit Chamber Music Festival was sponsored by the National Commission for Culture and the Arts (NCCA).

That festival showed off the range of possibilities that the Casa San Miguel was capable of. The week opened with the Bulgarian coloratura, Mariana Ivanova, as principal soloist. Frequent patrons of Manila's concert scene eagerly waited to hear the winner of the Madame Butterfly International Competition's interpretation of some familiar arias. Seated alongside the famous were the local youths. They were expectant too, but of what?

Miss Ivanova launched her program with *Casta Diva* from Bellini's "Norma" and a piano transcription of *Cara Nome* from Puccini's "La Boheme." The Manilans were appreciative, but the townsfolk were enraptured. What did these children of farmers, fisherfolk, vendors and clerks hear? What did arcane bel canto singing mean to them? Says Coke: "Music, all art for that matter, works on two levels. For those who have studied the form, a performance or exhibition goes from the senses to the heart and then to the mind. For those who are encountering it for the first time, it goes straight to the heart. Coming to a recital won't solve the problems these people will face tomorrow but at least for today they have been transported to a different place."

If the opening of the music festival was unusual for a rural venue, then the final performance weekend was positively demanding. It was a program featuring strings, primarily violins and cellos, that didn't fall back on the popular standards. Instead it opted for pieces by contemporary composers, such as Karl Popper's *Requiem* (a cellist's favorite) and Samuel Barber's *Dover Beach, Op. 3*, as well as some unusual pieces from the classical repertoire like the *Lento Asai* from the Beethoven *String Quartet in F-Major, Op. 135* and the *Piano Quintet in E-Flat Major, Op. 44* by Robert Schumann. It was a weekend of glorious, if often unheard music, and a stretch for performer and audience alike. Comments bass-baritone Emmanuel Gregorio, who sang the Barber piece: "It's a haunting work that begins in D Minor and builds progressively towards an impassioned finale in D Major. It is very difficult to sing, and I suppose, asks much of the listener as well. But I loved performing it and I believe the people loved hearing it." As if to give the audience a reprieve, the next piece was Claude Debussy's popular *Sonata for Piano and Violin*, performed by visiting American artists, Lydia Forbes (violin) and Dena Levine (piano). A crowd pleaser, the sonata is a virtuoso composition full of fiery glissandos and humorous motifs.

"Some may say our selections are a bit unusual, but we plan our programs to be interesting and artistically balanced," says Coke. "If a work of art has merit then the Art Center has a duty to play it, sing it, dance it or show it. We can't become a museum of 'old favorites.'"

Maintaining a balance between the original mandate of the Art Center as a creative cloister and the needs of the community had become a distraction for the Center's board. While some want to restrict available resources to "serious" art forms, others wanted to enlarge the venue to make it more accessible to the local residents and to paying patrons of the popular theater. "Because we are so new we seem to be constantly defining and redefining who we are and what our role should be," says Coke. "The townsfolk would like Casa San Miguel to stage a beauty contest, others would like us to showcase cross-over performers. [The Art Center did showcase Grace Nono]. High art, low art, no art... these are questions we are constantly facing."

As one solution, the Foundation has begun workshops and events designed for the community. Using the talents of visiting artists, they have set up a series of instructional seminars for groups of local children who, by talking to the artists and watching them go through the creative process, might see how an idea can grow into a finished work of art. "If we can just show these kids the path to artistic creation, perhaps one or two of them might even venture a first step," says Didi Dee, owner of Hiraya Gallery in Manila and the Casa's visual arts manager. To help them take those initial steps there are workshops in which the local youth can learn pottery, woodworking, *batik*, candle-making and stained glass design. "While we want to avoid becoming a 'livelihood' center, we are teaching some basic crafts so that the townsfolk can sell what they make," adds Coke. "But the fundamental question we are wrestling with is whether that is part of our original purpose or whether circumstances are pushing us off course." Yet, despite Coke's misgivings, these projects are showing some success.

WHILE THE Chamber Music Festival was in progress, as part of the Center's interdisciplinary approach to art, the Casa also invited visual artists Roberto Feleo and Brenda Fajardo and dancer/choreographer Myra Beltran to be featured artists. Their collective theme was the exploration of the Filipino sensibility through mythology.

Feleo displayed his critically acclaimed *Tau-Tao*, a three-dimensional visual retelling of the Bagobo myth of afterlife.

Using Feleo's work as inspiration and stage set, Myra Beltran created a dance in three movements interpreting the *babaylan's* (shaman) invocation to the deities of the spirit world. Fajardo's works also retold the lore of pre-Christian Filipinos, like the flight of a beleaguered Manobo clan and their search for immortality, but in a two-dimensional medium, painting.

The three exhibits were not only examples of personal achievement but also of the Center fulfilling its role. Casa San Miguel made it possible for three different artists, working in three different mediums, to share their vision of a theme with each other and with an audience.

Explains Coke: "There have been points in history when artistic ideas flowed across different mediums of expression, and it was at those points where some of the greatest works of art and important milestones in our culture were produced. I believe the driving force was proximity. During the Renaissance in Italy it was many different artists working for the same patron. Impressionism as a unified artistic expression in France owed much to the socialization in the cafés along the Montmartre. In America, the café was replaced by the university, notably Princeton and Columbia, where musical experimentalists like Otto Leuning, John Cage and George Antheil were able to interface with one another and with minimalist visual artists, while trying out new ideas. I am not saying a new renaissance will happen at Pundaquit, but wouldn't it be exciting to find out?"

Creativity isn't restricted to the invited artists. In the evening, the energy stoked by the day's events electrifies Capriccio, the Casa's outdoor restaurant. Beneath the mango trees everyone extends the artistic feast to the dinner table. In between bites, they exchange ideas, plan new projects, doodle on sketch pads or simply catch up on each other's works-in-progress.

THE ENVIRONMENT at the Center, though, is hardly all work and no play. There are fields to roam, chairs and divans set out under the trees for quiet moments and a lovely littie fishing town just a ten-minute walk away.

What does a soprano do when she isn't singing? At Casa San Miguel she goes to the beach. Which is what Mariana Ivanova and a group of painters and writers did the morning after the festival's first day. Setting out in five bancas, they headed for the Casa's private cove, a perfect spot to forget everything and just enjoy the sun, sand and water. "Let's dance," someone suggested. As if on cue, another started humming melodious passages from the ballet and Filipino folk songs, and the spirited, picking up the music, swayed and stepped to the beat. It was a finale reminiscent of a Greek movie. The characters having fulfilled their roles, all went to the seashore.

Wading through carabao plop in Pulilan

If every dog has its day, so must the carabao. And it does in Bulacan. It happens on May 14, when the beast of burden is first primped and then paraded down the main street of Pulilan during the annual Carabao Festival.

On all other days, the carabao of Pulilan, like its kin in any Philippine agricultural town, bears the yoke in the service of its master, the rice farmer. On festival day, however, the carabao claims its moment of glory: the serf turns lord, the farmer serves the beast.

We drove to Pulilan with our 14-year-old nephew Kiko in tow to watch this reversal of roles. That we didn't know a soul in town proved to be serendipitous. We thought the best place to ask about the festival schedule was at the church, and that's where, thank heaven, we met Rene Cruz. Rene was in charge of the church's decorations and when we came upon him he was attending to the last-minute details. He became, henceforth, Beatrice to our Dante. "I'll take care of you," he simply said, and off we went.

We were treated like long lost relatives. Since the festival was hours away, Rene took us around town and beyond, going as far as Calumpit Church, the oldest church in Bulacan. We also visited Malolos to see the Mololos Cathedral, built in 1817, and the Barasoain Church, where the constitution of the First Philippine Republic was written. In Apalit, located on the boundary between Bulacan and Pampanga, we visited the tin shops where craftsmen beat jeepney tin into baroque candlesticks, wall moldings, picture frames and mirror frames that are snapped up by Manila antique dealers and resold at huge markups.

Afterward Rene brought us to his home and plied us with food and drink like there was no tomorrow. Kiko, a city squirt, who is unused to the kindness of strangers, returned Rene's thoughtful gestures with an incredulous look. "What's the catch?" he asked, having been honed on Manila's quid-pro-quo ethic. "There's no catch," we assured him, "this is Bulacan."

THE CARABAO Festival is a folk-religious holiday celebrating the rice harvest and Pulilan's patron saint, San Isidro Labrador. Everybody turned out, including a group of Westerners who were ushered to a place of honor—a flatbed truck—for the best view. Most of the local revelers came in their Sunday finery. Young boys sported fresh haircuts, little girls wore their first rouge and grizzled farmers rallied to the occasion, looking awkward in their pressed slacks and dress shirts. But none looked more incongruous, if delightfully so, than the carabaos, who were beflowered, beribboned and besashed.

The entire town was "dressed up" as well, gleaming under a canopy of buntings. The church altar, besides being draped with the seasonal vestments, was also covered with bread, sheaves of rice, fruits and vegetables—offerings from grateful parishioners now enjoying a good harvest.

By one o'clock, the crowd along main street began to swell. The procession wouldn't begin until three, but everyone wanted to stake out their own space. We were lost in the press and getting a bit nervous about the darkening sky. We didn't bring umbrellas or extra clothes. What should we do if it rained? Rene laughed at our anxiety. Rain, apparently, was what the folk were praying for; even just showers would mean a festival doubly blessed.

Heaven soon obliged and the rain came. Not in sheets but in a gentle trickle like the light touch of holy water at a benediction. The crowd responded with glee as they received the blessing from above.

Soon, if not the sound of thunder then the sound of drums, synchronized and not so synchronized, shattered the quiet and the first school marching band came into view. The Carabao Festival had officially begun.

FOR THE next hour or so floats carrying representations of farmers, animals and saints made from woven vine passed through the throng of townsfolk and guests. School groups in bright native costumes performed folk songs and dances. Finally, the stars of the show, the carabaos, made their appearance.

Spectators who had been pressing toward the parade path and thus making it narrower, now jumped back. These were full-size beasts, very up-close and personal. Occasionally, one would stray from the center of the road and send the crowd scampering for safety. No one wanted to be gored or get their feet crushed under that awesome weight.

As each carabao passed the church it knelt on its two front legs, taking its cue from the farmer perched on its unsaddled back. Not all carabaos know how to bend their knees or when to bend them, but in Pulilan the farmers teach them well. And their skills surpass genuflecting, as they can walk several steps in that position.

Pulilan's clergy bestowed their blessings on each carabao from a position of comfort and safety on the church's upper balcony. As the last kneeling carabao made its way slowly past the church, the rest of the herd came thundering into town. Even though these carabaos hadn't yet learned to genuflect, they received a blessing anyway.

After the parade the food stalls opened and it was time for dining and dancing in the streets. The dining was a pleasure, the food fresh from the surrounding farms. The dancing was more problematic—the carabaos had left a legacy in the streets. Pre-curtain jitters, we concluded. Even beasts must wrestle with stage fright before they tread the boards.

In Obando 10 is not enough

When putting in a home entertainment center or taking out an appendix it's a good idea to follow the directions. At other times, though, well intentioned (but inaccurate) directions can lead you down a merry path. Our trip to Obando for the fertility dance festival was one of those times.

Our instructions told us to take the North Highway to Meycauayan, turn right and follow the road to Obando. However, after two hours on "the road to Obando" we began to think we were on the road to oblivion. Imagine our surprise when, having left from Caloocan, we started seeing jeepneys marked Monumento and buses that said Cubao and Alabang. It wasn't

Dorothy Parker's Vicious Circle or Walt Disney's *Circle of Life*, but the more familiar "going in circles"—we were practically home again.

In terms of kilometers, Obando, a fishing and farming community in Bulacan, is just a stone's throw from Metro Manila. Once you're on the MacArthur Highway, it is less than an hour from Valenzuela. Of course, considering Metro Manila's bizarre traffic, measuring distance in terms of time has very little meaning.

After traveling for what seemed like hours, all the while beseeching the intercession of Saint Christopher (old gods and some saints refuse to die), we finally arrived in time for the end of the day's procession and the beginning of the fertility dance.

OBANDO HAS been a pilgrimage site for almost 200 years. Hundreds of supplicants called *tuloy* (welcome ones) come to ask for divine intervention in finding mates and starting families, attracted by Obando's triumvirate of saints: Santa Clara, San Pascual de Baylon, and the Virgin of the Salambao.

Santa Clara was the childhood sweetheart of Saint Francis of Assisi up until he entered the religious life. She herself was eventually canonized for her purity and devotion. San Pascual was known for his love and protection of children. The image of the Virgin Mother was found in 1763 by two brothers, Juan and Julian de la Cruz, tangled in their *salambao* (triangular nets). They brought it to the priest of Obando, who had the image enshrined above the altar. The icon we see today is supposed to be the same one the brothers found, refurbished.

THE HISTORY of ritual dances and fertility rites runs deep in the Philippines and Obando is no exception. As in most early civilizations, fecundity was the desired trait—a good harvest, a generous sea and lots of children. Obando, formerly known as Catangalan (*amid the mangroves*), practiced the Tagalog ritual of *tadtarin*, a fertility dance for the *anitos* or natural spirits.

Catangalans, along with most Filipinos at the time, were also influenced by the Indian god *Linga*, a phallic representation of Shiva (Lingayen is named after this image). If the early Christian missionaries were to succeed, they had to accommodate these beliefs. In dedicating the Obando church to San Pascual de Baylon, they had a natural solution. "Baylon" can be loosely translated from the Spanish "*bailar*," meaning "to dance." Now instead of chanting the *diwang* and dancing for the old gods, the Catangalans could sing praises to Santa Clara and dance for San Pascual.

The origin of Obando's Christian fertility festival comes in at least two versions; one comes to us from oral tradition, the other from a reworked version found in Rizal's *Noli Me Tangere*. According to the older legend, only San Pascual was the patron saint of conception. A *suka* vender advised a childless couple: If they went to Obando and prayed to San Pascual they would have a baby boy. The couple went and when they looked upon the image, they discovered that the itinerant vender was in fact San Pascual. They had a child, but it was a girl. Disappointed by the child's gender, they punished San Pascual, by venerating Santa Clara instead. The tradition holds to this day, making her the ranking saint of the festival. In Rizal's novel, the same story is moved forward in time and embellished, the baby girl becoming Maria Clara.

THE FERTILITY dance is held inside the Obando Church on three successive mornings: May 17 in honor of San Pascual, May 18 for Santa Clara and May 19 to venerate the Virgin of Salambao.

The original church, built in 1754, was badly damaged during the Pacific War and has since been restored and renovated. The only original sections left are the exterior walls in the area behind the altar.

As we entered behind the procession, the church was full. Before proceeding to the nave, many stopped to touch their handkerchiefs to the faces of three saints. The supplicant couples gathered in the altar area, the rest of the town filled the pews and the aisles to cheer them on. The men, many dressed in *camisa* and *kundiman* pants, all had straw hats; the women wore *patadyong* and carried fans. When the crowd settled in, if not down, the Hymn to Sta. Clara began:

Santa Clara pinung-pino
Ako po ay bigyan n'yo
Ng asawang buenong-bueno
At anak na labing-walo
Santa Clara pinung-pino
Ang pangako ko'y ganito
Pagdating ko sa Obando
Sasayaw ako ng pandanggo
(Gentle Sta. Clara
Give me a good wife
Who will bear me 18 children
Gentle Sta. Clara
I vow that when
I arrive in Obando
I will dance the fandango)

Curious, we asked around—why 18 children? Surely just 10 would be enough for a full-court basketball game. No one knew. Eighteen it was and 18 it is.

THE HYMN and the dance are definitely Hispanic. The rhythm starts off moderately and bodies start swaying in place, hats and fans waving in the air, castanets clicking. Soon it picks up tempo and the dancers begin to move with abandon. The church takes on the energy of a revival meeting and the texture of a rock concert. It is a mixture of the bawdy and the beautiful. The congregation, now standing on the pews, are shouting encouragement to the supplicants while adding their own rather unique words to the hymn:

Santa Clara, pinung-pino
Ako po ay bigyan ninyo
Ng asawang labing-walo
Sa golpe ay walang reklamo
(Gentle Santa Clara
All I ask
Is 18 husbands
From whose beatings I won't complain)

In the modern Incarnation of the Obando Festival, children are not the only boon asked. Some of the men dance before San Pascual hoping to find a wife. The women may ask Santa Clara for a husband. Some come to ask for good health or prosperity. Others dance in celebration, a universal thanksgiving—for the harvest, for one's family, for one's faith. According to Fr. Rosendo Manolo Jr., Obando's Parochial Vicar and one of the four priests who lead the dancing, "Santa Clara stands for 'clarity,' '*claro*' in Spanish, and it is to her that I dance, thanking the Lord for giving me a clear calling."

One vestige of the "old ways" still remains. Sitting in front of the church's main door, elderly women sell small wax figures of men, women, children, and various body parts. Supplicants would buy a figure that most closely resembles what they're wishing for (a male figure if they want a husband, a torso if they want an ailment cured) and then burn it in a brazier as an offering.

"Does dancing at the festival produce results?" we asked. "Of course," the folk replied, pointing out all the children in the church who were conceived after their parents danced. They even have a name for them, the "Children of God." But, if we still doubted, the farmers and fishermen told us about the "professor," a doctor of obstetrics and gynecology in Manila, who comes with his wife each year to participate in the festival. As Father Jun said, "Surely, if this man of science believes, a miracle cannot be far behind."

Rites before the rites

Between Ash Wednesday and Good Friday, Pampanga, just north of Manila, becomes Calvary country. In this province of luxuriant rice paddies and sere lahar fields, where the signs of both God's charity and wrath are ever present, religious devotion runs deep. It seems everyone is busy preparing for the Lenten season—women in kitchens baking cookies, men in backyards polishing *carrozas* and children getting underfoot as clerics and laymen hang the church's mourning cloths. All this activity is accomplished amid the eerie wail pouring out of speakers mounted on chapels or window sills. In barrio after barrio, the Lenten season is here, the *pabasa* has begun.

Vaguely resembling a muezzin's call, the ritual singing of the Passion sounds different in each barrio. It is "jazz" in its most classic definition. The modal chant, to which the words of the Passion are set in the local dialect, has never been written down. Some chapters of the versified text, which starts with an invitation to the people to join in the singing and ends with the prophecy of Christ's Second Coming, are sung with a universal melody line that has survived through tradition. The rest is improvisation, each singer inventing a melody that he or she feels is appropriate to the meaning of the words.

If the voices sound ancient, the reason is that most of the singers in Pampanga are elderly. Yet despite their many years, there is strength and fervor in their delivery. In the tradition of minstrels, Pampanga's small band of devoted *Pasyon* singers will spend the Lenten season moving from place to place, vocalizing Christ's suffering.

Demetrea Catu, 82, has been singing the *Pasyon* during Lent for 67 years. As a young girl of 15, she learned it by listening to her elders. As she sits in the Lacsamana home in Mexico, Pampanga, holding a microphone and squinting at the *Pasyong Mahal*, she looks up smiling and says, "I am lucky. I can still see the text. The older folks, who can no longer see well, must do it from memory. It is a privilege that the Lord has allowed me to tell His story and I vowed I would continue to sing the *Pasyon* until my very last Lent on earth."

MEANWHILE OTHER Pampangos have been working and planning for weeks and months for their turn to show their devotion.

Sitting by a window in the dusty *barangay* of San Vicente in Mexico, Abelardo Capili creates the 296-page *Pasyon* books. In the tradition of the 12th century scribe-monks, about whom he knows nothing, he works at a tiny desk adorned only with a blotter and a master copy of the text he will transcribe. Each book is hand-lettered at the rate of four pages a day. It will take *Apu* Abelardo three months, using only a drafting pen, to finish a single book, which he will sell for P3,000.

A carpenter by vocation, he is a calligrapher by avocation. But, it wasn't until he was working in Guam in 1962 that he was able to put his self-taught skill to use. "The Filipino community wanted to organize a *pabasa* but didn't have a book. I had mine, but it was worn out, so I made a copy for them. Before long, more and more people requested copies." To date there are 70 of his books in existence and no one knows how many more will be produced. *Apu* Abelardo is 82 years old and doesn't have a protegé. "None of my 10 children are interested in what I'm doing," he says with regret.

Francisca "Paquita" Mercado Lising is also busy. An energetic woman of 85, she is opening several locked wooden boxes. Treasure chests, they hold the rich costumes that will be worn by her family's religious icons in the Good Friday procession. Like a magician, she pulls wonder after wonder from the boxes. White satin cloths embroidered in gold thread. A tiara of beaten silver. A gown of purple crushed velvet emblazoned with silver trim. She proudly unfolds the *carroza's* skirt, yards of white crochet that she made herself. The months it took her to finish it are reflected in the quality of the workmanship. She will also sew the small pillows that are laid around the *Santo Infierno* during the procession. The cloth and lace used to make the pillows have been donated by her neighbors. After the procession she will give the pillows away as a talisman.

In the middle of her sala, *Apu* Paquita dresses the image of Mary Magdalene. Her wrinkled fingers, relying on the experience of 68 years, deftly fold the unwieldy lace veil around the icon. When she was younger, *Apu* Paquita also took care of the family's two *carrozas.* Now the task falls to her daughter Lillian.

The *carrozas* will be rolled out of storage to be cleaned and polished until the silver gleams and the wood reflects the deep beauty of its many years. On procession day, their crystal *viriñas* will be installed and the platform covered with fresh flowers.

The images and the *carrozas* have been in *Apu* Paquita's family for as long as she can remember. With a pride borne of piety she points out that when the town procession begins on April 14th, three of the 12 images will be hers.

ALTHOUGH AT times it may seem otherwise, the devotional activities in Pampanga are intensely personal. Regardless of how theatrical they appear, they are never "theater." Nowhere is this truer than among those devotees who are crucified or who flagellate themselves.

Roland Navarro, director of the penitents in barrio Cutud in San Fernando, spends the year organizing the *penitencia* and screening applicants. "I tell those who wish to be crucified for the first time that what we do is not a joke. The five-inch nails are real and the pain is real. Between the time they make their vow and Good Friday they must prepare both their bodies and their minds through prayer." Although potentially dangerous, nobody has been maimed in the 32 years Navarro has been in charge of the ritual.

Every year there are between eight to 13 crucifixions and about 600 flagellants. Navarro notes that with few exceptions, the penitents are not atoning for sins but rather beseeching divine intervention. "Most are taking the vow of crucifixion or flagellation in the name of a sick parent, spouse or child," he says. A penitent, once accepted, must undergo the ritual for at least 10 years. Many make it a lifetime commitment.

Among the penitents this year will be a man from Belgium. Says Navarro: "We are attracting a lot of attention in Europe, America and the rest of Asia. I have received letters all year round from foreigners who wish to take part. If they are sincere, they are welcome. Our rituals are open to all."

In addition to the *penitencia*, Navarro also organizes a street play in Cutud recalling Christ's Passion. The play, which covers the period from Christ's sentencing before Pontius Pilate to the Crucifixion, was written by Navarro's father and is acted out by the town's residents.

As spectators, actors or penitents, everyone in the tiny barrio of Cutud takes part in the Lenten festivals.

THE PRE-LENTEN Pampango rituals at Crescencia Cabral's house center around the kitchen, where she is baking her San Nicolas cookies. Flat, thin and embossed with the image of San Nicolas, these Easter treats resemble a medieval medallion with serrated edges. "This cookie mold is at least 100 years old," she says, holding up a 5" x 7" woodblock made of *kamagong*. For its size it is surprisingly heavy. "I inherited it from my mother, who got it from her mother."

Making San Nicolas cookies is a specialty of Mexico. No one remembers when or how the tradition started or why it honors San Nicolas, since the town's patron saint is Santa Monica. The only explanation the folk could offer is that San Nicolas, a 13th-century Italian priest, fed the poor with bread he made himself.

The original San Nicolas cookies were made from arrowroot, imported butter and carabao milk. Because they were fragile, they were stored in clay pots which were then hung from the ceiling to prevent ants from getting at them. In those days, the cookies were baked only during special occasions, particularly Easter, and served to the family or given away as gifts.

Today baking San Nicolas cookies has become a cottage industry. "A very modest one, really," says Crescencia, who has been making them in limited quantities since 1975. "Now they can be enjoyed year-round, although naturally, our largest orders are placed during Easter."

For commercial purposes, the bulky clay pots have been

replaced by cardboard boxes, and the original ingredients modified. Flour is used instead of arrowroot and margarine is considered healthier than butter. In many homes in Pampanga, however, women still grow the rootcrop in their backyards and use the old recipes.

For the elders of Pampanga, the San Nicolas cookie might be considered a bellwether. They say that change is coming to Pampanga. Slowly, but surely. They have come to accept that traditions must be modified or they will die. Despite this realization, the old bemoan the fact that the younger generation isn't learning the old Lenten rites that have kept the family and the community together for generations. Betis is an example. In the past, before Vatican II, townsfolk held a Lenten rite unobserved elsewhere in the Philippines. They turned Betis church into their own version of Calvary where the church's religious images were crucified so that they may share Christ's suffering.

Fortunately, there are still enough youngsters who feel strongly about the old ways. Crescencia Cabral has a coterie of teenage kitchen aides who are learning to bake San Nicolas cookies. A 17-year-old boy in Mexico is being groomed as a *Pasyon* reader. And throughout Pampanga there will be pageants and plays that involve entire *barangays*, children and ancients, each with a role to master during the Lenten season.

Just as Holy Week proves the Church indomitable, in Pampanga it proves folk traditions indestructible.

Bogies at 12:00 high

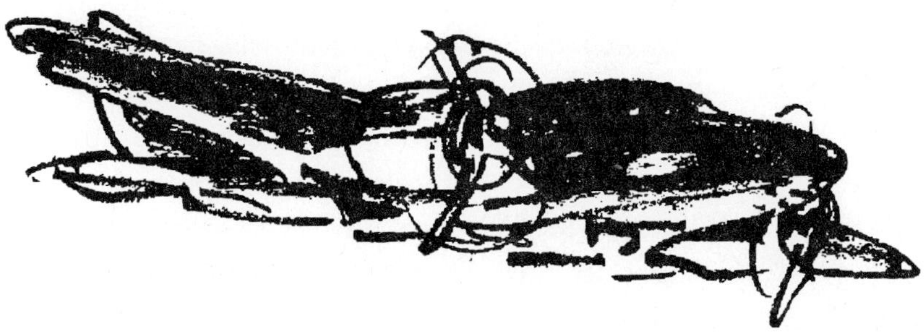

"... [The] four pieces of equipment that most senior officers came to regard as among the most vital to our success... were the bulldozer, the jeep, the 2-1/2 ton truck and the C-47 airplane."

~GEN. DWIGHT DAVID EISENHOWER

Seen on the ground with its tail on the tarmac, its nose in the air, and its oversized wings spread out like Dumbo's ears, she looks rather frumpy. But looks can be deceiving. During World War II, the C-47 Skytrain, nicknamed the "goonie bird," was also called workhorse, dependable, beautiful and, frequently, hero.

Able to take off and land on just 1,200 feet of runway and "treetop" at a ground speed of under 90 mph, the Skytrain was used for just about every type of mission. It was a flying truck carrying munitions, food, jeeps, tractors and anything else that could be squeezed into the cabin; a flying hospital that could get in and out of places other planes couldn't; a paratrooper transport; and a personnel carrier. Its simple design was also a wartime asset. Not only can the C-47 fly on one engine, it can glide with no engines to a safe landing. To the pilots it seemed indestructible. When a C-47 was bombed in Suifa, China, the wing was shattered and the fuselage riddled with shrapnel. Yet the plane had to be moved lest it fall into Japanese hands. Improvising, the crew fitted out the stricken plane with a smaller wing from a DC-2 and managed to fly their "DC 2 1/2," shrapnel holes and all, out of harm's way.

Many veterans agree that if it hadn't been for the C-47, the Allied offensive in the Pacific might have ended before it even started. When the Allied troops landed on Guadalcanal in August 1942, the American Navy could not maintain supply lines. It fell to the Airforce to fly in supplies from Espiritu Santo Island, a 1,300-mile round trip which had to be made without refueling. Obviously a job for the Skytrains, which performed it with routine efficiency.

In the Philippines, Skytrains were used to bring in troops to Luzon and paratroopers to Corregidor, landing them with extreme accuracy on a tarmac cut short by the sea cliffs. During the invasion of Leyte, Skytrains brought in 22.5 tons of quartermaster items, 70.6 tons of ordnance, 7.2 tons of medical supplies and 1.5 tons of communications equipment to support the ground troops.

TODAY, TWO fully restored C-47 Skytrains are back in the Philippine skies. This time with a gentler mission, flying passengers to isolated beach resorts and other holiday destinations.

"You don't do this for money, you do it for love," says Captain Danilo Crisologo, who pilots one of the two planes. "Our company spent months doing research so that everything about these planes would be authentic. We even found the original paint for the fuselage, U.S. Military Shade #41, a dark olive drab."

From the vintage 1940s Ray-Ban sunglasses and Coca-Cola

advertisements painted on the airplane's nose to the military insignias on the fuselage, the two planes are exact replicas of the fleet used by the 317th Troop Carrier Group that operated in Leyte in 1944. "You see these planes housed in museums," Captain Danny continues, "hanging from ceilings by cable wire, or as miniatures in glass cases, but have you ever seen one fly? We have taken a page out of aviation history and brought it to life."

For Captain Danny, sitting in the cockpit and looking through the four-paned "V" windscreen, it is like being in an Errol Flynn movie. Outfitted in a jump suit with authentic 5th Army Airforce patches, he cranks up Glen Miller on the plane's sound system, kicks over the two Pratt and Whitney engines and lines up on the approach path at Manila's domestic airport amid the sleek 737s for a flight back in time. Of course, the 737s will soon be roaring above the clouds at 30,000 feet with a ground speed of 600 mph while his Skytrain will be bumping along at 10,000 feet and 130 mph, but to the Captain, that's real flying.

And most pilots and air buffs agree. When one of the Skytrains landed during a recent airshow, two MIG fighter pilots who had been demonstrating their high-powered jets to members of the Philippine Air Force, came over and practically demanded to be taken up. Or as Daniels MacLain, who first flew a C-47 in 1948 and is still flying a DC-3, puts it, "I would rather fly a C-47 than make babies."

On the C-47 the 30 passengers behind the pilot sit side by side on canvas jump seats along the walls of the fuselage. Overhead is the cable that was used to hold the static lines when paratroopers occupied similar seats. "If you merely want to get there, take a commercial flight," says Captain Danny. "But if you want to dream, come with us."

As the plane goes up and the cabin temperature goes down, who among the passengers doesn't imagine he is sitting alongside Glenn Ford or Gregory Peck, holding an M1 rifle and a picture of the girl back home. It's fantasy at two miles up. One day soon the fantasy will start even before take-off. "We want to build a Quonset hut for our loading terminal to complete the scenario of the 1940s," says Captain Danny.

The boarding area is now in the modern Avia Terminal at the Old MIA Circle. Still the illusion is preserved as preflight passengers listen to recordings by Jo Stafford, Tommy Dorsey and the McGuire Sisters or watch old World War II movies like *Objective: Burma* and *Dive Bomber Pilot*. There is also a good library in the waiting room on the C-47 as well as the original service manuals. When it's time to board, instead of the usual signboard at the gate, the "let's go" signal is a vintage recording of *In the Mood*. Once on the plane, passengers can help themselves to 1940 editions of *Time*, *Newsweek*, *Life* or *Esquire*. Snacks are served in K-ration boxes.

BUT A PLANE can't fly on nostalgia alone. A closer look at the Skytrain's cockpit reveals that the 1940s is only skin deep. Although the controls are authentic, as are the windows, all those vintage dials and levers are hooked up to state-of-the-art equipment. "We maintain the Skytrains like a Swiss chronometer," says Captain Danny. "Each plane routinely undergoes a maintenance schedule that exceeds aviation regulations." The C-47, he stresses, is one of the safest planes ever designed. "When they built these warbirds they didn't have the equipment to measure tensile strength or any of the new space-age metals we have now, so they just used the very best of what they had and built each plane with loving care." In fact, the overall safety and service record of the DC-3, the civilian version of the C-47, created such a demand that it became the most widely produced transport plane in aviation history.

The Skytrain's two senior pilots are veterans. Crisologo is an air transport economist with 20 years of flying experience. Captain Ding Deang, the other pilot, is a former Air Force officer and Philippine Airline pilot who has logged over 29,000 air-hours.

THE TWO C-47 Skytrains made their debut at the 50th Anniversary of the Leyte Gulf Landings in October 1994. One of the planes worked as a shuttle between Mactan Island and Tacloban while the other provided aerial tours of the battle sites and took part in the vintage airplane fly-by.

Since then, the Skytrains have been operating as charter planes and offering half-hour aerial tours of Manila for P450 per passenger during the dry season. Says Captain Danny, "We offer adventure travel. When we fly to Boracay, for instance, we take the plane down to 1,000 feet and skim the island before we land in Caticlan. We have flown parties over the crater of Mount Mayon and Mount Pinatubo, and to Itbayat, the most rugged island in Batanes. We've also provided skydivers with a sense of what the paratroopers must have felt jumping from a C-47. As a charter company, we can go anywhere, anytime. It's all up to the passengers."

TO CRISOLOGO, the C-47 is as much a part of Philippine history as Corregidor or Bataan. To ensure its rightful place alongside our other war memorabilia, he is hoping that the two restored airplanes will be declared National Treasures by the National Museum to make sure they are preserved for generations to come.

The walls of history

For the explorer, the thrill is to step where no man has walked before. For the archaeologist, historian and curator it is to stand knee-deep in the footsteps of others, seeking to find out how they got there and why. Intramuros is the domain of the latter. The oldest part of Manila, it has been occupied and modified since Rajah Soliman established his fortress settlement, Maynilad, on the banks of the Pasig.

Intramuros is living history. Despite wars, man-made alterations, natural disasters and neglect, it is still possible to touch the same stones that a Spaniard touched in the 16th century, to walk in his footsteps along the wide walls, or to stand beside a cannon where a long departed Japanese soldier stood, searching for American invaders to come from what is now Manila's tourist belt. When peering into the ancient dungeons at Fort Santiago and then kneeling at the altar in San Agustin Church, one knows that the man who held the jail keys knelt at the same altar. In Intramuros, amid beauty and death, you are living both sides of the human equation.

The elaborate carvings, bas reliefs, ecclesiastical masterpieces in the churches and a rich commercial and social life that set the trend for the rest of the archipelago notwithstanding, Intramuros was built for war. Its walls were meant to keep people out and at various times they did; often as not, they didn't. Soliman's bamboo fort was reduced to splinters by Spanish cannons, but the Spaniard's reinforced perimeter couldn't keep out the Dutch. England breached the barricades in 1762, as did the Americans in 1898, although it was a mock battle since Spain had already accepted defeat. In later years the walls, which were built to stop musket balls, proved no match for 102-inch guns and mortars, and the city cited by King Philip II of Spain as "Distinguished and Ever Loyal" was decimated by both the Japanese and American forces.

The job of picking up the pieces finally fell to the Intramuros Administration (IA), created in 1979 by Presidential Decree 1616 to rehabilitate the 67-hectare fort and the contiguous area outside the walls known as the "buffer zone."

ALONG WITH the renewed interest in Intramuros and the restoration work came three mysteries, one of them already solved. *MYSTERY ONE:* This dates back to World War II and resolved itself just a few years ago. An American treasure hunter, Charles MacDougal, convinced the Philippine government that the fabled Yamashita treasure was buried in Fort Santiago. With official permission, he brought in heavy earth-moving equipment and began to dig. After an exhausting hunt that wore out everyone's patience, the result was, no treasure was found. All that did happen was that the weight of the machinery and MacDougal's haphazard digging caused a historic vault to collapse. *MYSTERY TWO:* When restoration work began in earnest, IA staff members went to Spain to research the original building plans of Intramuros. As expected, they found the paperwork pretty much corresponded to what they had been uncovering back in Manila. Except a large tract in Fort Santiago that wasn't on any site map. They now think that it was a secret arms foundry, but not enough evidence has been forthcoming to make a positive identification. They need to dig deeper. *MYSTERY THREE:* The most stubborn of the three mysteries begins in the mid-1500s and is yet to be unraveled. In 1978 IA diggers uncovered what appeared to be the base of a towerlike structure at Baluarte de San Diego. It has three concentric circles bisected into quadrants. Subsequent research proved that the bisecting walls were an addition to the original structure. But what was the original structure? Could it have been part of the very first Intramuros stone fort, the Nuestra Señora de Guia? "Yes, it could have been," replies Architect Rene Luis Mata, IA senior historic sites development officer. "But why in tight concentric circles?" Another theory is that the builders wanted to enlarge the first circle, so they built around it. But then why didn't they knock down the walls of the first circle before putting up the second one? Another explanation is that, like the mystery site in Fort Santiago, it too was a foundry. The site had been referred to in the past as *funducion*. But again, Mata says, not enough material has been found to substantiate the allegation. The theory that it was once used as a cistern is probably correct, according to Mata, since some of the stones bear traces of a terra cotta overlay for waterproofing. But the cistern was a later structure—and a short-lived one. So what was its primary use then? Says Mata: "Anybody's guess right now is as good as anyone else's."

IN ADDITION to mysteries, Intramuros also holds a number of surprises. Just when you think you know her, there is more to learn. The Puerto Real, for instance, is the main gate to Intramuros. It was used for all state occasions and by the governor-general. However, there are two other gates which have a more interesting past. The Postigo del Palacio, built in 1783, has alley-ways to the palace of the governor-general and the residence of the archbishop. Either could use it when they wanted to leave the encampment unnoticed or bring someone in without attracting attention. Jose Rizal was taken from his cell in Intramuros to Rizal Park for his execution via this gate. Another gate, Puerta del Parian, was used exclusively by Chinese and native merchants who were not allowed to enter the fort. They would have to leave their merchandise at the portal and Spanish soldiers would bring it inside.

Among the many things that Intramuros contained, one was a *corrida de toros*. It was located in Plaza Roma, then known as Plaza Mayor. The bullfights were held up until 1773 when the wife of the new governor-general converted the *corrida* into a garden. When the Americans came, the garden remained but was renamed Plaza McKinley. It only became Plaza Roma in the 1960s when the Philippine government signed a reciprocal agreement with the Church, which also established a Plaza Manila in Vatican City. Incidentally, the bronze statue of Carlos IV in the Plaza was not put up by the Spanish but by the Philippine government in 1824 as a "thank you" for sending the first small pox vaccine to this country.

While some Intramuros plazas are steeped in heroic history, one is steeped in a historic scandal. Plaza Sampalucan is reputed to have been the original site not of a plaza but a love nest. The house was built in 1621 by a Spanish merchant as a meeting place for him and his lover, the wife of the governor-general. Once discovered, they were both executed by the cuckolded husband and the house demolished. The site remained an empty lot for years, shunned as being both haunted and sinful. It didn't become Plaza Sampalucan (named for its *sampaloc* trees) until 1980.

Trompe l'oeil paintings are only a surprise if you don't know they're paintings. But when they are as well done as the paintings in San Agustin Church, they are worth seeing again. The oldest stone church in the Philippines, San Agustin is a treasure trove of ecclesiastical art and architecture. In addition to their fine museum, of special interest is the elaborately carved main door, the baroque pulpit, the molave choir loft and the 18th century pipe organ.

WITH THE major renovations complete, most of the current work in the historic district is new construction. Mata points out: "All new buildings have been designed to suit the period of the place and observe height requirements as well. While it is restrictive, few developers protested because the beauty and importance of Intramuros raises the value of their properties."

IA was also part of the building boom. They put up a 25-room hotel in Plaza San Luis, across the road from San Agustin Church. Set in three colorful townhouses—green, pink and blue—each facade represents the architecture of a different province. Green is Taal, pink is Iloilo and blue is Vigan. The hotel's public rooms are decorated with period furniture.

FROM AN abandoned area used primarily by squatters and 10-wheel trucks racing to the port, Intramuros has become a tourist destination. Now under the auspices of the Department of Tourism, the original City of Manila hosts some 1.2 million visitors a year, most of them locals. Concludes Mata: "Intramuros is a part of our heritage. While we are delighted to share it with the rest of the world, Intramuros essentially belongs to and should be used by Filipinos."

Speculations on a neighborhood enigma

When traveling, we expect to learn something new about people, places and things. We have guidebooks to help us meet these expectations and guides who fill in the local color. But then there is the circular foundation at Baluarte de San Diego inside Intramuros, opposite the Manila Hotel. It's in the guidebooks and if you go there you can arrange for a guide. But if you are hoping to add it to your list of "things I learned on my trip," you can't.

A signboard by the entrance says: "*The circular structure is one of the oldest constructions in Intramuros, originally designed in 1586 by a Jesuit priest, Father Antonio Sedeno. Begun as a circular fort called Nuestra Señora de Guia, it was renovated in 1593 and incorporated into the city walls. In 1644 a new bulwark, the Baluarte de San Diego, was begun, enclosing the older fort.*" Unfortunately, according to recent research, most of the information on the sign is wrong!

Scientists from the National Museum and the Intramuros Administration (IA) who work at the site now agree that the circular foundation is not one of the oldest but the oldest structure in Intramuros. But that's all they agree on. As for it being designed by Father Sedeno or it even being a fort, that's speculation and neither the IA nor the National Museum will confirm those theories until more information is uncovered through further diggings. The problem is, they can't dig any deeper because the already brittle foundation might cave in. They need special probing instruments, like X-ray and sonic imaging machines, which the government will never buy, at least not for projects of this kind.

So, here stands the ruins of a massive construction, laid out in three concentric circles bisected by lateral walls, built in the late 1500s, and nobody can absolutely say what it is. In fact, since the 1970s the site has been poked and prodded by archeologists and historians, architects and travel writers, with the end result being—your guess is as good as the experts'.

In addition to not knowing what it is, they don't even have a name for it. The triangular bulwark which contains the ruin is the Baluarte de San Diego, while the ruin itself might or might not be the Nuestra Señora de Guia. So some call it the "foundation" and others refer to it as the "Baluarte." We think the most appropriate name would be "enigma."

A close cousin to this ruin would be Stonehenge in England. Like our mystery here, Stonehenge is a massive construction sitting in an incongruous surrounding, a suburban pasture. But unlike the Baluarte de San Diego, science has nibbled away at its secrets. Where once it was also an enigma, we now know that Stonehenge is a ritual and agricultural calendar. At the Baluarte we have a mystery which is still holding its own with other mysteries, such as the disappearance of the dinosaurs and the Mayans. Actually it is faring better than those two. Experts now think that a comet did in the former and a drought the latter.

Although the mystery behind Stonehenge is gone, it is just as imposing as before and it certainly remains a miracle of early engineering. But it has also lost something intangible—its power to astound.

The engineering that went into the Baluarte is no less imposing. While the rocks aren't nearly as large as those that make up Stonehenge, the craftsmanship with which the walls were assembled is remarkable. Each stone was cut to be a perfect fit with its surrounding blocks. By contrast, the lateral walls, which were built at a later time, are more haphazard, depending on the mortar to keep them in place.

ALTHOUGH WE move around Manila a lot, we ashamedly admit that like so many other Manilans, we have paid little mind to Intramuros. We only went to the Walled City to fulfill a travel assignment, an easy one, or so we thought. However, when confronted by the Baluarte de San Diego, we knew we couldn't simply zip in and zip out. There was more to the site than just a historical puzzle.

We have stood before many ruins on several continents, but this one seems to have a strange aura about it. We never put much faith in astrology or ESP. Yet since we saw it, that ancient structure and the aura it emanates have been in our thoughts. If it turns out to be some sort of runestone or a witches' graveyard we would not be surprised.

Life in 16th century Europe, when the Baluarte was built, was replete with magic, witches, warlocks and spirits. If England could send their witches to America to be burned in places like Salem and Lowell, Massachusetts, isn't it conceivable that the Spanish government sent their *brujas* to the Philippines—a sort of "out of sight and out of mind" solution?

It's also possible that, unlike the English in America, the Spanish soldiers here, far from home in a pagan land, decided that some spells cast by friendly Spanish witches, in conjunction with their faith in the Church, might help them safely reach the end of their tour of duty.

Another difference between colonial America's experience and our own is that witches in the Philippines, like priests and healers, have always been part of the native way of life. The folk respected their powers and, in much earlier times, regarded them as spiritual leaders. Among the Filipinos with whom the Spaniards were interacting, one maltreated a *mangkukulam* at great peril to oneself.

In this type of environment it is totally understandable if the Spaniards equated their own witches with the local *mangkukulam* and rather than persecute any of them, treated them with respect and even assisted them in their Sabbaths. What kind of assistance could they render? Perhaps building an edifice in which the coven might practice their rites. The shape of the structure supports such a theory, as three concentric circles make up a powerful symbol in European occultism.

In which case, why is it referred to as a fort even in early manuscripts? Because, in all probability, as far as the missionaries knew (and they are the ones who wrote the manuscripts), the officers and conscripts were building a fort. In 16th century Europe it was common to build double- and triple-walled forts where the livestock were kept inside the outer wall. (There are still a number of double-walled forts in Indonesia, a leftover from their Dutch colonial days.)

So the Sabbath site was built, if not in absolute secrecy, at least with its purpose shielded from those who might disapprove. It is interesting to note that when a group of Filipino scholars went to Spain to examine the architectural plans of Intramuros, they found every structure in the Walled City meticulously detailed. Except two. A munitions foundry (fairly well documented through current excavations) that the Spanish considered a military secret and the structure at Baluarte de San Diego, which is only referred to in passing. Obviously, if they were building a coven site they wouldn't send detailed information back to Spain where witchcraft was considered heresy.

Then you might ask, why are there no local records of strange goings-on? First of all, in a land of *babaylan* and *mangkukulam*, the goings-on might not have been considered so strange. Second, who would have kept them? Filipinos couldn't enter Intramuros unless they worked there and most had to leave by nightfall when the Sabbaths would be held. The few who remained inside the gates must have had either very trusted positions or were doing extremely menial jobs. Both would be expected to hold their tongues.

ACCORDING TO European folklore, where witches meet the land dies. Perhaps that explains why, when the Spaniards later tried to use Baluarte de San Diego as a cistern, the water wasn't potable. It was contaminated by salt. In fact, since the first Spanish conquerors built it, the Baluarte has resisted being used for anything other than its original purpose, a Temple of the Black Mass. Stranger yet, in a walled city where space is always at a premium, this large and strategically sited area was simply abandoned.

We think the residual effect of those Sabbaths has yet to evaporate and you can feel it for yourself if you go there.

BUT IF you don't like our theory of witches, you don't have to buy it. You can go to Baluarte de San Diego and play "guess the function" too. You might even come up with a better explanation. You merely have to incorporate three "givens" into any theory: It is the oldest structure in Intramuros. The concentric walls pre-date the laterals. At one time it held water. That's it. You're up to speed. Now, does anyone want to make a case for extraterrestrials?

Phoenix rising

Even at night the sky above Manila Bay was blood red, probably in sympathy with the blood that flowed on the ground below. It was April 12, 1942, three days after Bataan had fallen, when the Japanese concentrated all their long-range guns on Corregidor. From their occupied positions in Bataan and from Cavite, supplemented by air raids, the Japanese unleashed a merciless barrage against the "fortress" in Manila Bay. Seeking shelter from the shells that fell like rain, President Manuel L. Quezon, Vice President Sergio Osmeña and Chief Justice Jose Abad Santos joined American General Jonathan Wainwright and 14,000 Filipino-American soldiers and civilians in the miles of tunnels beneath The Rock.

Most of the Allied gun emplacements facing Bataan were destroyed less than a week after the initial Japanese attack. Those facing Cavite and Manila were in no better shape. Reveling in their victories, the Japanese marked Hirohito's birthday on April 29th by intensifying their attacks, completely destroying Battery Geary. By the fifth of May, the first Japanese ground forces landed on the tail of the tadpole-shaped island, at Infantry and Cavalry Points. It was the beginning of the end.

At 10:00 a.m., on May 6th, the last day of Allied resistance on Corregidor, the front line was less than 180 meters from Malinta Tunnel, the Command Headquarters. Lookouts reported the Japanese had already landed tanks on the island. Lacking anti-tank guns and aware of the damage those tanks could do inside the tunnels, General Wainwright said, "The end must surely come tonight. It is better [for it] to happen in the daylight."

Exactly at noon, a white flag was hoisted at Topside as Wainwright left the Malinta Bunker for Denver Hill to meet with his rival, General Masaharu Homma of Japan. Wainwright spent the remainder of the war as a POW in Sian, Manchuria. He survived, though, eventually sitting with General Douglas MacArthur at the signing of Japan's capitulation at the end of the war in 1945.

CORREGIDOR ISLAND lies 42 kilometers from Manila and 6 1/2 kilometers from Bataan peninsula. Together with four other islands—Caballo, Carabao, El Fraile and La Monja—it traditionally guarded the narrow opening to Manila Bay. While its strategic importance in the defense of Manila has become obsolete, its historical importance is greater than ever.

The early sea traders knew Corregidor as Marbella Island, a pirate's lair, providing excellent cover for the Moro freebooters who sacked those unfortunate vessels they managed to catch.

The origin of "Corregidor," the island's present name, which means "corrector" in Spanish, seems in doubt. Some believe it came from the fact that Corregidor was used as a customs checkpoint for Manila shipping. Others believe the name is derived from a former Spanish penitentiary ("house of correction") on the island.

Historically, the strategic value of Corregidor seemed apparent to whomever occupied it at the time. The Spanish partially fortified the island with gun emplacements. The guns were insufficient, however, to stop Admiral George Dewey in 1898. The Americans, building upon the early Spanish arsenal, thoroughly fortified the island, adding bomb shelters and 23 elaborate gun batteries. Now a dedicated military encampment bristling with armament, Corregidor became known as The Rock.

Whether Corregidor was ever a really good fortress is moot. The pirates couldn't hold it against the Spanish, the Spanish couldn't stop the Americans, the Allies, despite considerable preparations, couldn't fend off Japan and finally, Japan couldn't hold off the Americans as they retook Corregidor in March 1944. Still, although it might be an inept citadel, Corregidor has proven a superior tourist attraction and a shrine for World War II veterans.

TOURING CORREGIDOR Island is not a nature tour because most of the island's natural beauty has been blasted away. It's not an architectural tour either, because the architecture has been blown away too. Maybe it's a morbid curiosity tour, visiting a moment of history at its bloodiest. A Disneyland of Death. We found it incongruous to watch our boatload of Westerners (we saw very few Filipinos on the ferry), in their loud "tropical" clothes, eager to arrive at a chunk of real estate that in previous years so many other Westerners were equally eager to leave.

For touring purposes, Corregidor has been divided into two historical zones. The head of the island, known as the Topside and Middleside, where most of the ruins and gun batteries are located, has been conserved as the Memorial Zone. The Tourist Zone covers the Bottomside, the Malinta Tunnel and the Tail.

Most tours start at the Filipino Heroes Memorial just beyond the ferry dock and then follow a series of internal roads leading to all the "sites of interest." An impressive plaza, the Memorial contains 14 larger-than-life bronze reliefs that depict the Filipino's struggle for liberty. It starts with the Battle of Mactan (1521) and ends with the EDSA Revolution. In the center is a dedication which reads, "To the Filipino who knows how to die for love of freedom and liberty." Behind the plaza is a small museum containing a collection of outstanding old photographs of Filipino heroes and historical events.

Along the same road there is a mini-botanical park, the Japanese Garden of Peace. It became the center of controversy when the Japanese installed vintage WW II cannons on the site. Many felt that cannons, even defunct ones, were not really an appropriate "peace" symbol.

The next stop on the set tour is the first authentic relic, the tunnel complex. Moving farther towards the "head" of the island is the famous Malinta Tunnel. This was the stage upon which the early war years played out. A labyrinth of 24 lateral passages and 12 sublaterals, it was the temporary seat of the Philippine government, the Allied General Command headquarters and probably the largest subterranean hospital in the world. The hospital is also unique: it was never designed to cure sick people. Its 1,000 beds were occupied by healthy young men whose bodies had been torn apart by shards of metal.

In 1976, National Artist Lamberto Avellana and sculptor Napoleon Abueva designed a 30-minute sound-and-light show inside the tunnel, using actual props and life-size bronze statues. As the show began with thuds and smoke and sirens, our group, standing in the semi-darkness, bellied up to each diorama ready to experience the sights and sounds of agony—in complete safety.

Beyond the Malinta Tunnel is the Memorial Zone on Topside, the highest point of the island, where the ruined buildings of a once thriving community have been left just as they were 52 years ago. Driving by the old YMCA, the barracks complex, including "Mile Long," the officers quarters and the base cinema, is an eerie experience. All are twisted and charred, no longer resembling buildings but rather sculptures from hell. It is hard to believe that people once lived and played in those structures.

Further on are the gun batteries: Hearn, Geary, Crockett, enormous structures, intricately engineered. Although their bunkers are shattered and the guns are all pockmarked from strafing and small arms fire, to the untrained eye they look as though they could be fired up all over again.

Amid the debris there is a new structure, The Pacific War Memorial, built by the US government in 1968 at the cost of $3 million and dedicated to the Filipino and American soldiers who died on Corregidor. Working with astronomers, the designers erected a circular chapel covered by a marble dome that has an opening at the top. Every May 6 (the day Corregidor fell) at exactly noon, sunlight falls on this opening, creating a spotlight on the circular commemoration altar below.

An adjacent mall contains marble panels on which are engraved the major battles fought during the Pacific War. Beyond the mall rises a wing-like steel sculpture symbolizing the Eternal Flame.

Alongside the memorial is another museum containing artifacts found on Corregidor after the war. Boots, buttons, dog tags, letters and personal photographs. Like the barracks, the artifacts put a human face on war. Here is a picture of a fatally wounded young doctor who lived long enough to write his own death certificate, there several mahjong tiles charred at the edges. It is a museum of the mundane.

The renovated 19th century Spanish Lighthouse offers the tourist a bird's-eye view of Corregidor. The climb is not difficult and well worth the effort. In the mall in front of the lighthouse is a mileage post: Manila, 26.6 kilometers; San Francisco, 6,972 kilometers; Tokyo, 8—. The rest is defaced. Someone neither forgot nor forgave.

Peninsula of icons

"There's Calatagan," the captain said, pointing to a tongue of hilly land in the Verde Island Passage. We were on the bridge of the Super Ferry on our way back to Manila from Cebu. It was our first glimpse of this Batangas town.

What caught our eye was a lighthouse. We had passed it on our way out, but it was midnight and all we saw then was a beam of light radiating from somewhere, indifferently scanning the darkness. Perhaps that's how a lighthouse works: it's not supposed to find you, you're supposed to find it.

And find it we did on the return crossing. A tall, white, slender structure rising from the meadows, looking as majestic as the blue mountains beyond.

We found that lighthouse again, a year later, when we drove to Calatagan. This time, though, it wasn't just an anonymous light source seen from the deck of a ship. It now had a name— Punta de Santiago Lighthouse—and a proud history. Since it became operational in 1890, no ship in the area has ever run aground.

Up close, the ancient lighthouse sheds its austerity and becomes a part of the rustic landscape—of the hills and the beaches, of the bougainvillea, flame trees and *kalachuchi*, of the goats that chew on the grass and the dogs that chase the goats and the children that run after the dogs. It is also part of the people's lives: when asked for directions to the structure, they say, *ang parola 'ga?*, referring to the lighthouse in the old, familiar Spanish term, and then proceed to tell you the way in their sing-song Batangueño accent. (Manilans who speak the same Tagalog never sound this delightful.)

THE PUNTA de Santiago Lighthouse is a good place to start an exploration of Calatagan, a peninsula on the southwestern tip of Batangas province. It is an area of increasing historical and archaeological importance. Early excavations along the southwestern coastline in Balangan yielded traces of human habitation dating back to 250,000 years. Among the most remarkable of these relics are rough-cut stone figures called *likha*, representations of supernatural beings that early Filipinos created to serve as messengers to the deities of the skyworld.

The settling of Calatagan, according to oral tradition, goes back to the 13th century, when 10 Bornean chieftains fled the tyrant Makatunaw. They sailed northward to the Philippines, landed on Panay in the Visayas, then spread out in search of other settlements in the archipelago. Two, Dumangsil and Balensusa, reached Balayan Bay. From there, they made their way inland down to the shores of Taal Lake.

With their families and their slaves, they set up a self-contained community. They grew rice, wove cloths and, being literate and skilled in the art of government, soon exerted leadership over a wide area composed of what are now the provinces of Batangas, Oriental and Occidental Mindoro, Quezon, Laguna and part of the Bicol Region.

This territory was known as Bombon, and its wealth drew Arab, Chinese, Annamese and Indian merchants. The lively trade carried out in the area through the centuries is evidenced by the artifacts dug up in Calatagan.

The area became a mecca for amateur archaeologists and collectors when the National Museum uncovered pre-Spanish gravesites containing large quantities of Asian trade pottery in the seaside barrios such as Kay Tomas and Pulung Bakaw. Among the enthusiasts in the "Calatagan Pot Rush of 1959" were National Artist Leandro Locsin and his wife Cecilia. "The digging fever had swept the coastal barrios," they wrote in their book, *Oriental Ceramics in the Philippines*. "Farmers, who ordinarily plowed the land listlessly, suddenly found themselves with eyes glued intently to the ground for signs of broken pottery." Stumbling on a grave site meant earning a fast buck as pottery literally became a cash crop. Farmers and fishermen hawked artifacts as they would fish and vegetables. Ming pottery was sold by the basket, strung-up ancient glass and carnelian beads by the bunch. Instead of rice cakes, roadside venders pressed celadon jars and plates on motorists.

The Locsins joined in, not entirely for the booty—they already owned a sizable collection of Asian pottery—but for the excitement of the dig. They chose to explore a village aptly named Hukay (*hukay* is Tagalog for pit). In just one month of excavating, the Locsins found 27 whole and broken pieces, mostly pottery from 14th to 15th century China, Siam and Annam, along with stone axes, metal implements, beads, spindle whorls and net sinkers. They were all valuable, but not nearly as exciting as their first find: a Ming celadon bowl.

The Locsins' forays into barrio Hukay enriched their lives in another way quite apart from their cache of pots. It brought them face to face with the folk of Calatagan who "overwhelmed us with their kindness." Each weekend the Locsins returned to Calatagan, they were "bombarded" with fresh fish, crabs, the best there was. They reciprocated by flying in ice cream bricks and popsicles.

WE EXPERIENCED the same kind of Calatagan hospitality on our short visit, too. Upon hearing of our fascination with old houses, our driver Roger, a native of Calatagan, offered to take us to a neighbor's home, which he described as "interesting." The neighbor turned out to be Ricardo Baylosis, an interior designer and antique dealer whose clients include the Zobels. We were merrily on our way to Ricardo's house when Roger hit the brakes. The car that just zoomed past us also stopped. The two drivers greeted each other. It was Ricardo, on his way to get a haircut. There goes our old house, so we thought. But Ricardo said, "just knock on the door and tell my sister I invited you."

We did. We weren't only let into the house, we were shown its every nook and cranny, including the master bathroom where, instead of the usual plastic drum most Filipinos use for storing water, Ricardo has a large Chinese jar embossed with dragons. Entering the house's central court, we went down to a sunken rock garden, using steps made from half-buried stone grinders, the kind the old folk used to make rice paste. At the center of the garden we found an altar of *likha*. Throughout the house, Ricardo had transformed heirlooms into new pieces, such as a handloom ingeniously converted into a hammock.

After touring all the rooms, and taking dozens of pictures, we thanked the lady for receiving, us and left. Only later did we realize that not only were we perfect strangers to her, we didn't even learn her name.

CALATAGAN USED to be one huge *hacienda* and forest preserve owned by the Zobel-Ayala family. Although they have sold most of their landholdings, you can still feel their influence on the town. Our guide recited the litany: "This is where the Zobels play polo, there is the runway and hangars for the Zobel company airplanes. The cattle farm and horse farm belong to the Zobels and that is the Zobel mango orchard."

We weren't sure if the Zobels had something to do with the flock of roosters crowing their lungs out at the gamecock farm by the highway. But at the town center, there's no mistaking you're in Zobel country. The main streets are named after members of the clan, and in one spot, right where the Calatagan Church is, you'd find yourself standing on the corner of Zobel and Zobel.

On a knoll inside the Zobel *hacienda*, Don Enrique Zobel, now confined to a wheelchair because of a riding accident, has built a handsome building without stairs. It was meant to be a gift to the Tahanang Walang Hagdanan, a foundation for the disabled. Somehow the turnover didn't push through and the property is now used as a retreat house under the care of the Don Bosco community. Close by, on another knoll, he built a lovely chapel dedicated to San Isidro, the farmer's patron saint. It, too, has no stairs and the sides are completely without walls. The pews are made of split pine logs, the ceilings lined with *sawali*. Hanging above the altar is a larger-than-life statue of the Crucified Christ, the work of a Spanish artist named Talavera who also painted the tiles depicting the Stations of the Cross. Both buildings are simple but elegant, a Zobel trademark.

The showpiece Zobel property is, of course, Punta Baluarte, a leafy resort, carved out of a rocky cliff and patterned after the best resorts found on the Costa Brava in Spain.

You would think that having lived in the shadow of the Zobels this long the Calatagan folk would come to resent their influence and power. Nope. The people of Calatagan speak tenderly of the Zobels. "When Inigo, Don Enrique's son, got married," they recall, "there were two receptions. One at Punta Baluarte for guests from Manila, the other in town for the entire Calatagan community. Don Andres Soriano, one of the *ninongs*, brought in truckloads of softdrinks and Magnolia ice cream for everybody. We had a fiesta."

The folk probably don't realize it, but the best treat they got from that grand wedding was the full renovation of the Calatagan Church where the rites were held. No one could tell us when it was built—all the folk could say was "*kinagisnan na namin*" (it's been there since we were born). They know for sure, though, that Don Alfonso Zobel built it.

Not familiar with the Zobel genealogy ourselves, we couldn't place Don Alfonso's time. But judging from the church's architecture, it must have been erected in the mid- to late 1800s or early 1900s. Anyway, the date matters little. More important is what the small church signifies.

On the church patio there is a stone cross richly carved with religious figures. The carver, no doubt, was well schooled in the pantheon of Catholic saints, but he was also an adherent of a much older faith. At the base of the cross rests a *likha*, from whose crude form springs, in totem-like fashion, the more recognizable cast of Christian icons. So long as the cross stands, the people of Calatagan will always remember their past.

The restoration of Pagsanjan

Reputation is a fragile thing. It can be lost through the malice of others, by accident or by negligence. Fortunately, it can also be restored, though the process can take years and a lot of painstaking work.

Pagsanjan had lost both its reputation and its heritage. For many years its reputation was that of a modern-day Sodom. Its infamy was such that, although Pagsanjan had everything a municipality could want to qualify as a key tourist attraction, the Department of Tourism dropped it as a recommended Philippine destination.

It took the dedicated effort of the town's hoteliers, merchants and the local government to clear Pagsanjan's name. The discos and beer halls were closed and the pedophiles informed in no uncertain terms they were no longer welcome. Today the private sector continues to repair Pagsanjan's image.

Restoring the town's grand houses, the showcase of Pagsanjan's heritage, is being attended to as well, but by far fewer people who are less financially endowed. They seem, however, to have substituted dedication for their monetary shortfall.

Anthony Page, who has turned a youthful enthusiasm into a cause, is a leader of a loosely formed group of local architects, artists and designers who want to turn Pagsanjan into a living museum. "Like Intramuros or Vigan, Pagsanjan has a unique character," he says. Or as native daughter Gilda Cordero-Fernando wrote in an essay about the town of her father and grandfather, "[Pagsanjan] was a town that had a passion for a comfortable and a cultured life."

In that same essay she recalls a time when the Yangco Steamship Company ran boats from the Pagsanjan River to Laguna Lake and then into the Pasig River. Passengers would disembark close to Escolta, the premier commercial street of Manila. This easy access to Manila made Pagsanjan a trade center, raising the town to a position of superiority over its neighbors.

Although Pagsanjan has fallen on hard times, its passion for culture and comfort is still discernible as you drive into town beneath the two lions that stand on the welcome arch over Calle Rizal. The houses on the main street still put up a facade of stateliness although many have been grossly altered on the inside. The large elaborately carved windows and doors, the balconies, the gates, all bespeak a place and a time when the *dons* ruled their families and their town with a patrician reserve.

Page was born in Pagsanjan and studied architecture in Manila. He is single-handedly undertaking the first of a series of restoration projects, the Cordero ancestral house. Says he: "This house is typical of many of the great houses here. There is enough of the original house to work with, but there is an awful lot of work to do." He is starting with the restoration of the facade. Once that is done he will then move inside. "While much has been changed over the years, the floors are still original, as is the coffered ceiling in the main sala," Page points out. "Even the wooden grill work and the architraves (the elaborately carved triangles over the beams framing the windows) that are now hidden beneath layers of paint are original. This house will be brought back. But it will take time since we have to move more carefully, using old pictures and reference books to ensure the accuracy of our restoration."

The Rivera house up the street is even older than the Cordero house. According to the owners it was built in the mid-1800s. However, despite its being over 200 years old, it still has a lot of the original furniture and the rooms still retain their original configurations. "This is the home of Leonor Rivera, Jose Rizal's sweetheart," our guide told us. Nobody else we met could confirm it. We found out later that Rizal met his true love, who was later immortalized in fiction as Maria Clara, in Intramuros and that she was a native of Pangasinan, not Pagsanjan. But, since we are not historians, merely romantics, we would like to believe it was *her* house we were visiting.

Adding to the problems of restoring Pagsanjan to its former glory is that the town was badly damaged during WW II. Pagsanjan was repeatedly carpet-bombed by Allied raids, destroying much of the rich architecture. Yet, enough of the old homes remain, and there are enough people like the Corderos who still care, to give credence to Anthony Page's efforts.

Page and his Group of 10 (the name is as informal as the group) are getting support mainly from homeowners, merchants and the provincial council. They are now looking into the feasibility of re-zoning the area as a historic district and eventually turning it into a tourist attraction. Already shops like *Arte de Santiago*, an exclusive Filipiniana boutique which occupies a refurbished grand house on Calle Rizal, are blending into Page's vision to create a new-old town of the *dons*.

The grandest house in this town of grand houses has got to be the house of God. Pagsanjan Church was founded in 1687 by Agustin de la Magdalena as a bamboo and nipa structure. The stone Spanish colonial building was built in 1690 and the transept was added in 1872.

The Church is a treasure chest of local religious art, each icon unusual. The Santo Intierro here wears a richly embroidered *salumbaba* or death scarf; the Santo Niño's breeches are tucked into silver cowboy boots; a life-size Virgin Mary stands on a crescent made of carabao horns; a second image of Mary is holding a giant rosary.

WHILE ANTHONY Page hopes to use history and culture as a magnet to bring in tourists, the number one attraction in Pagsanjan is (and will probably continue to be) the river and the falls. People come from all over to board colorful bancas and be swept down the river and up under Magdapio (Pagsanjan) Falls.

But like the town, the river and the ride were controversial.

The river was becoming brackish through abuse. Unlicensed *bangkeros* were charging innocent tourists as much as P1,000 per person for the river-run, way over the regulated rate of P250 per person. The very economy of Pagsanjan was being threatened.

These problems are now being solved. Legitimate tour operators and the hotels facing the river are lobbying the city for stronger ordinances while they are spending their own money to clean up the waterway and publicize Pagsanjan as a destination for family outings. Among the plans is lighting up the riverbank at night and landscaping Calle Rizal from the arch to the church.

Pagsanjan is also receiving influxes of new money as Manila-based hotel chains are opening resorts in what they hope will be a bustling vacation region.

Another area under development is the lush terrain above the Falls. Easily accessible, it is about a half-day excursion from the major resorts along the river. George J. Salvador, a resort manager who has made the trip, says: "You go by jeep to barrio Cavinti, the jump-off point. From there it's a 15-minute hike on an improvised road to Nakulo Falls. There is no strenuous climbing involved. Any reasonably healthy person can do it and the reward is breathtaking." By now it was obvious we were speaking about something he loved as his words came tumbling out. "It's called Nakulo Falls because the water pressure is so strong it seems as if the water is boiling. Above the main falls [Magdapio], which everyone sees from the river, are two terraced falls that are the feeders. Up here the walls of the canyon are black, caused by water erosion. You have a panoramic view of the river below and there are wild monkeys and kingfishers which occasionally come out of the surrounding woods to keep you company. When ready, it will be a whole new area of an old tourist attraction, breathing with new life."

Gilda Cordero-Fernando concluded her essay by lamenting the passing of the grand houses, the traditions and the landscape. Residents like Anthony Page, resort manager George Salvador and the faceless executives from Manila's grand hotels who are bringing in new investments to the area may eventually give lie to Gilda's complaints. A new life for this tired tourist attraction is long overdue.

The magical town below the magic mountain

Remember Brigadoon? That mythical village in Scotland which materializes from the mist only one day every hundred years? Majayjay must be its sister town. The town has been on the map every single day since it was founded in 1597, but when the temperature dips, by five in the afternoon, the fog rolls down from Mount Banahaw and the entire town disappears. Shrouded in the icy mantle, it sleeps, invisible to the world, until the warm morning sun chases the fog back up the mountain and reveals the town once again.

On a trip to Majayjay you sense the magical atmosphere of the place long before you reach the town. The road from Los Baños to Magdalena seems to be strewn with fairy dust. "*Te amo verde*," sighs the land, its lushness increasing with every kilometer. Green is the color of ricefields, of sampaguita hedges, of great acacia trees rising from both sides of the road, their branches interlocking to form a living ceiling.

As in a dream, expect the unexpected. Somewhere in Magdalena the railroad tracks end at someone's front door. What happens when the train comes? Before your question is answered something else springs into view. The mountain that towers at the end of the road bears down on you like the landlocked Colossus which once bestrode Rhodes. It is Mount Banahaw, the holy ground of amulet makers, faith healers, soothsayers and seekers of things divine.

Majayjay is at the foot of this mystic mountain. One enters it via a centuries-old bridge spanning a lovely river, one of many lacing the ethereal Laguna town. This particular river forms a V, its two arms cascading down the mountain and creating a pool beneath the bridge. Women do their laundry here, sitting midstream on rocks in the shade of makeshift huts, the waters gurgling around them. If you saw this scene in a painting, you would dismiss it as too saccharine, too idealized. Yet there it is, as real as the larger-than-life statue of the Nuestra Señora de Portiera that serenely stands on the riverbank. We wonder if she is the patroness of the *lavandera* or a reincarnation of an older goddess who once ruled the river spirits.

From the Virgin's grotto, the road climbs up small hills, twisting and turning, divulging one treasure after another until it reaches the greatest treasure of all, Majayjay.

IN THE late 1500s the area encompassing Majayjay was granted as an *encomienda* to Gaspar Osorio de Moya, a soldier who arrived in the Philippines with Miguel Lopez de Legazpi. (He susbsequently rose through the ranks to become one of the early mayors of Manila.) As such it is the oldest settlement in Laguna, to which at one time, the northern towns of Luisiana and Magdalena belonged.

By the 17th century, Majayjay was already famous for its church, one of the oldest in the Philippines, making it a popular tourist destination. At that time travel from Manila was quite complicated, involving a boat trip up the Pasig River across Laguna de Bay and a ride on a hammock borne by native bearers up the slippery hillside to the town. Yet despite the hardships, Majayjay hosted Manila officials and guests, including some European crowned heads. Governor William Howard Taft, a traveler during the American period, was so taken by Majayjay he ordered a road constructed from the town to the falls of Botocan. Visitors in those days stayed in the *convento* or in the fine stone houses along the main street.

Today, journeying to Majayjay is an easy drive over good roads, though lodging is a problem. The *convento* is now a school, and while the elegant ancestral houses are still here, they seldom open their doors to strangers. It's not a question of hospitality, it's merely a reflection of the times.

AS IN the past, visitors are drawn to Majayjay because of its church, an excellent example of Philippine colonial baroque. Rebuilt twice and restored three times, its walls are three layers thick, the result of "sandwiching" the original walls between new coatings of brick and mortar on both sides to strengthen them. Unusually tall for a Philippine church, it measures 16 1/2 meters high at the nave. The central aisle is 60 meters long, 17 meters wide and has long cantilevered balconies on both sides which lead to an enormous Franciscan cupola surmounting the altar.

But there is more drama to Majayjay Church than just architecture. It is a repository of folk memory. The first stone church was built in 1606, an undertaking that caused tension between Franciscan missionaries and the locals they used as slave labor. After a fire destroyed the first church, the population moved beyond the town boundaries to avoid being drafted again for building duties. The friars, obsessed with erecting an edifice in whose "utmost grandeur... the natives might recognize the majesty of the deity," chased down the villagers, burned their huts and forced them back to town. The present structure was completed in 1660 by a congregation coerced into bringing sand and gravel whenever they attended church. They were also compelled to quarry stones, fell and hew timber, manufacture bricks and lime, and put the church together block by block. Violators were flogged or fined. The hatred spawned by these acts eventually led to the division of Majayjay into three towns and, ultimately, to open revolution in 1896.

In more recent times, the not quite dormant animosity between priests and parishioners flared once again. Since 1988 Majayjay Church has been systematically divested of its treasures. The grand chandelier gracing the altar is gone, as are some church silver, and 11 of the 14 magnificent wooden reliefs carved by a local artist. Talk around town says the pieces were sold by the parish priest, ostensibly to pay for restoration work. The chandelier alone was worth the price of a brand-new Mercedes Benz, which was what an antique collector had once offered in exchange for it. Although the town brought the priest to court, nothing became of the case. The Church intervened, claiming the artifacts belonged to the diocese and not to the State. Now a solitary lightbulb dangles above the altar where the chandelier was, the three remaining reliefs are kept locked behind iron bars and the silver has been stashed somewhere in the *convento*.

Yet despite the continuing conflict, Majayjay Church remains a source of folk pride. The structure's primitive quality echoes the elemental beauty of the land and pays homage to the pains-taking labors of its builders.

JUST BEYOND the stolidity of the church is the chaos of the market. Where the church stands alone, in this part of town there is no notion of "aloneness." This is downtown Majayjay, all 60 square meters of it. Pedestrians vie with tricycles which compete with jeepneys for an empty patch of road. Venders fill every square inch of roadside. Even the dead are thrown into the commercial hubbub as the street level of the town's funeral parlor is occupied by stalls selling slippers and pots. Yet, if you push through this block-long knot of people and goods, once again you are confronted by empty, hilly streets gazing out on Laguna Bay and the mountains of Banahaw and Cristobal.

In Majayjay you are never too far away from a river. However, like the roads least traveled, the rivers hardest to reach are the loveliest.

Depending on weather conditions, you might need horses to get to Olla River. It is immediately identifiable by the central pier, a huge stone bridge jutting out of the water. It is the unfinished project of Father Victorino del Moral, Franciscan priest of Majayjay in the 1850s. The bridge was to be a short cut to the town. Called *Puente de Capricho* or Bridge of Whims, its name probably alludes to yet another priest's taste for grand infrastructure—at the expense of others. Like the builders of the church, Father del Moral's parishioners suffered for their prelate's enthusiastic engineering. Bridge-building duties were compulsory and malingerers were birched, which probably explains another colorful local name for the bridge, *Tulay Pigi* or Buttock Bridge. Perhaps because of his unpopularity, Father del Moral was removed from Majayjay in 1859, before his bridge was completed.

Father del Moral would be happy to know that his bridge and the Olla River have reached a kind of immortality—in film. Some scenes of the movie *Apocalypse Now* were shot here.

Unfortunately for Father del Moral, the original wooden sections on each end of his bridge were blown up in the film. The crew built a replacement bridge further upstream.

The road to the Botocan Gorge is well paved, but you need an official letter from the mayor's office to enter the area, as it is the property of the National Power Corporation (NPC). Despite the red tape, it's well worth the effort; once you're there you will be rewarded with a spectacular and unusual cable car ride.

The cable car, in operation since 1923, spans a chasm 600 feet wide, and goes down—it's also an elevator—the same distance to bring you to the NPC power plant at river level. The ride across and down allows for a tier-by-tier view of the jungle gorge. As you slowly descend you see two mountains overgrown with a double-canopy forest (notice the wild *rambutan* trees), the playground of hundreds of butterflies and swifts. Beneath you, slowly rising to meet the gondola, is the rapidly moving waters, sculpting out a snake-like path around the huge rocks in its way.

Taytay Falls, located in a valley on the southern foot of Mount Banahaw, is equally breathtaking. The trip down is arduous: a 20-minute drive from town, then a 20-minute hike to the picnic site and, finally, a 10-minute walk along the shoulders of an irrigation canal.

The three-tiered falls is a more rustic version of the better-known Pagsanjan Falls. It's also more pristine as the site doesn't lend itself to tourists who come by the busload. The falls empty into a deep, cold pool surrounded by the forested mountain walls. Further upstream lies the fabled Dagat-Dagatan Lake, also known as *Tubig ng Sinukuan*, because the surrounding vegetation seems to arrange itself in a kneeling position, as if in surrender.

Unlike Pagsanjan Falls, it costs practically nothing to enjoy Taytay Falls. The gate fee is extremely nominal, and you can camp out for as long as you want, provided you bring your own equipment and supplies.

BACK IN Majayjay, a short distance from the church, is an *ermita* dedicated to the Nuestra Señora de Portiera. According to lore, the chapel has a secret tunnel with two laterals, one leading to the Majayjay Church, the other to Mount Banahaw. The legend predicts that in the near future, the waters surrounding Laguna will rise and submerge the area. Only Mount Banahaw will be saved. At that same moment a church of gold will emerge on Banahaw's summit. Because the people of Majayjay have access to the tunnel, they will survive the flood.

When this happens, Majayjay, like Brigadoon, will vanish and who knows when it will come back to life again?

Town of sweet dreams

With the advent of the rainy season, unless you can get to drier places, you are left dreaming of blue skies and white beaches. A place like Puerto Galera. A dream-like destination that, in fact, fulfills sweet dreams.

Located on the northern edge of Mindoro Island, 130 kilometers south of Manila, Puerto Galera is a town comprising coastal villages arranged in a circle, broken at three points by a narrow channel. Landward, it is bordered by Mount Baco and Mount Masimbo, which lead up to imposing Mount Halcon.

Secured by natural seawalls on all sides, Puerto Galera has

always been considered one of the finest natural harbors in the Philippines as well as being one of the most beautiful ports in the world.

Your dream of a sunny island-world begins as you approach Puerto Galera through the Verde Passage. First you sail past a number of glittering coastal towns, then make a sharp turn into a narrow channel. As you emerge, the scene opens onto a tropical cove. You have reached your goal.

Even before you step on shore you can tell this place is different. Look at the sail boats tied to their moorings. These are not the "Sunday" boats of a posh yacht club. These vessels have been around, some coming from the farthest corners of the world. They belong to sailors home from the sea.

Over the years, Puerto Galera has become home for many of life's sailors too. Burned-out executives who traded in their business suits and pocket pagers for sandals and shorts, backpackers who never had pocket pagers or pockets to hold them, retired Europeans who now have a deep tan covering their fair skin and inveterate tourists who chanced on Puerto Galera because "it was there" and leave it with a deliberate promise to return. Such are the people of Puerto Galera.

An Englishman talks about life before and after Puerto Galera. When he retired five years ago, he looked around for a place to "rest his tired bones." Someone suggested Puerto Galera; he gave it a try. He planned to stay two weeks, but lingered for two years. After that he packed everything he owned and moved in permanently. "I'm content," he says.

In 1978, Brian Homan, a native of Sydney, figured in a diving accident for which he felt responsible. Like a Conradian man atoning for his "sin," Homan wanted to transport himself to a place where nature's cleansing energy could wash the guilt out of his soul. "I chose the Philippines, because I thought it was something like Fiji," he recalls. But when he saw Manila, he was disappointed. It was Sydney all over again. If he wanted Fiji, he was told, he should go to Puerto Galera. He did. And he is still there.

It's been more than a decade since Chuck Hogan cast off from his native Louisiana in search of the anchorage of his dreams. He piloted *Misty*, a 36-foot sailboat, down the Gulf of Mexico across the Atlantic into the Mediterranean Sea and disembarked in Greece. Continuing his journey, he headed for the Pacific and its exotic ports of call. Since he reached Puerto Galera he hasn't raised anchor once. "This is it," he says. "I found my paradise."

A WHILE back, Puerto Galera acquired a reputation for drugs and girls. But for the natives and the lost, those aren't its appeal. It's attraction is the way Puerto Galera seduces the senses by overwhelming them with sheer beauty. Here it is possible to tune in without having to turn on. There are more than a dozen white sand beaches packed into just 23,347 hectares. Some are large enough to contain a full-size resort, others barely big enough to hold six sunbathing bodies. Beyond the beaches are the mountains—green, deep and unfathomable. Above the mountains is the blue sky and wisps of white clouds. Who would want to leave?

Fortunately some people do leave, or Puerto Galera would be as jammed as a mall on a weekend. Every day the ferries come in full and leave full. These are the tourists who, like the settlers, have discovered a "faraway" vacation spot just three hours from Manila. You see husbands, wives, children unsteadily getting into bancas heading for the family resorts that are mushrooming around Muelle Bay. Here they will find a host of activities on land, sea and beneath the sea.

Hiking has become a big sport in Mindoro. One of the most sparsely populated and undeveloped islands in the Philippines, much of Mindoro is virgin land. Hikers set out for the mountainous interior on paths hacked out of the rainforest. Each step forward is a step backward in time. And just when you would feel "jungled out," the trees might part to reveal a primordial waterfall cascading down into a cool natural pool.

The mountains are also the home of the Mangyan, their small villages clinging precariously to the slopes where they eke out a subsistence economy through farming and by selling their tribal craft, such as the *ambahan*, ritual songs and love poems incised on bamboo sticks. On special occasions the Mangyan might come down to Puerto Galera, but usually you have to climb the mountains to meet these elusive people.

For the most part in Puerto Galera, the sea is the vacationers' playground. Every day boats go out with sports fishermen looking for tuna, shark and other pelagic fish, which abound in the waters. Closer to shore are the snorkelers, wind surfers, water skiers and swimmers.

Scuba is the number one sport and there are 30 spectacular registered dive sites. Medio Island is known to scientists all over the world for its rich marine life. The Canyons is the destination favored by experienced divers looking for adventure. Just to get there, you must first swim through a hole in an underwater wall which has to be cleared of soft corals and fish, and then pass through a cavern that is the lair of two-meter reef sharks. The canyons themselves are full of ravines, so take care not to fall into oblivion.

IT IS ironic that the very place where people have come to drop out and live close to nature should be sitting on a gold mine. Literally. The name Mindoro derives from *mina de oro*, or gold mine. While almost all rivers emptying into Mindoro Strait are gold-bearing, commercial mining is limited to the areas around Subang River and Madaan River. The reason is that the quantities found in the other rivers are too small to make mining there worthwhile. But, if like Dobsey in *Treasure of Sierra Madre*, you come down with gold-rush fever, beware, there's pyrite (fool's gold) in the river too.

Serious treasure hunters do come to Mindoro, but they don't look in the rivers or under the ground. They look under the sea.

More than a thousand years ago, long before the Europeans came to Southeast Asia, the Philippines was already trading with its neighbors and many of these ancient traders passed Puerto Galera. As early as 600 A.D., Chinese junks exchanged their cargo of pots, gilded ornaments and silks for Mindoro's gold and exotic wild life.

When the Spaniards arrived in the 16th century, they found Puerto Galera was an ideal shelter for their fleet of great ships from tropical storms. They called this profitable and snug harbor Puerto Galera or Port of the Galleons. From 1575 to 1826, Puerto Galera became a regular port of call of the galleon trade. Twice a year, galleons laden with Chinese tea, silks and porcelains, Indian cottons and carpets, Ceylonese gems and Indonesian spices crossed the treacherous Pacific from Manila to Acapulco, and returned filled with Mexican silver.

As one would expect, some of these vessels and their treasures went down. Folk knowledge as well as old Spanish texts tell how they sunk—and where.

Today, the man to see about a treasure-hunting expedition is Brian Homan, who runs Capt'n Gregg, a dive center on Sabang Beach. In 1983, while spear-fishing in one of Puerto Galera's channels, Homan accidentally turned over an oddly-shaped rock on the seafloor. The rock was in fact a Chinese jar, with dragons emblazoned on its sides.

Since then, Homan has been working with the Philippine National Museum to recover historical artifacts from wrecks off the coast of Puerto Galera. Among his finds: Sung and Ming porcelains; the remains of a Chinese junk; cannons that once guarded the decks of a Malay pirate ship; an amphora from the Spanish galleon, the *Nuestra Señora de la Vida*, which was lost off Verde Island in 1621; and, of more recent vintage, relics from a Japanese patrol boat, the *Irako*, sunk by the Americans in 1944.

WHAT IS Puerto Galera? A dazzling memory for a rainy day? A place to lose your past and not worry about your future? An affordable resort vacation on a white beach, wife and kids by the pool and you out with a snorkel? Is it also sitting at a dockside hotel with an ice-cold beer, watching people go by and ships load up? And at night, is it a starry sky, scampering house lizards and a hundred fireflies? Yes! It is all of these and more. In Puerto Galera there are no clocks and fewer rules. It is where imagination and reality meet in a town of sweet dreams.

Above and below ground in Palawan

As we groped our way across the muddy floor, we heard constant rustling, shrill squeals and the flapping of featherless wings. High overhead the sky wasn't blue—it wasn't even the sky. We were deep underground in the third chamber of Guri Cave, part of the Tabon Cave Complex, completely surrounded by bats and rock. It was our introduction to the other Palawan.

When one hears "Palawan" the first thing that comes to mind is El Nido, its alien landscape a beacon to tourists from all over the world. But there is another Palawan, this one with a topography equally bizarre and just as beautiful. It is the Palawan mainland, a long slender island that contains the capital city, Puerto Princesa, and pulls together all the satellite islands that compose the archipelago. Using Puerto Princesa as our base, and forsaking the banca for the jeep, we are heading inland, traveling north and south on Palawan's sole provincial highway.

OUR FIRST excursion is to the Tabon Caves, the cradle of Philippine civilization. Archaeologists Robert Fox and Manuel Ma. Santiago led exploration work in these caves between 1962 and 1968. Their outstanding finds, including the Tabon Man and the Manunggul Jar, both declared national cultural treasures, are now housed at the National Museum in Manila. During their initial excavations, they concluded that some portions of the yet unnamed caves had been disturbed by the Philippine mound builder or tabon bird, hence the name—Tabon.

Setting off at six in the morning, we are soon jostling on a dusty road to the seaside town of Quezon on the westernmost tip of the island. There we board a large banca (in Palawan you can never really leave the banca behind) for a short ride to the cave-island. Unfortunately the sea is too rough for the large boat to reach shore and we must switch amid the swells to a canoe. We plan the transfer carefully, hand over our shoes and bags to the canoe's *bangkero*, then step gingerly from the large boat to the smaller one so we will remain dry. Although our movements are well choreographed, the waves have a mind of their own and we are drenched. We couldn't be any wetter if we waded to shore. Which is what we decide to do.

Waist-deep in the water, we behold the isolated island spread before us. Except for a lonely eagle hovering above, there is nothing animate in sight. The caves set high up in the rock face look out upon the water like empty eye sockets. Yet man was here thousands of years ago and once we come ashore, we see traces of his passage everywhere.

Lipuun Point is honeycombed with more than 200 caves, of which 29 are considered to be of archaeological value. The 104-hectare area is enclosed by limestone domes separated by deep chasms. The age of the caves is placed at mid-Miocene or about 17 million years old and are believed to have been occupied by early man some 40,000 years ago. We also discovered that, despite our first impression, these caves weren't dead at all. Stalactites and stalagmites continue to grow in the caves, and bats, sea birds and swallow swifts are the new tenants.

The climb to the Tabon Cave Complex, which starts from the beach, is fairly easy. The National Museum has built a series of concrete steps and walkways connecting the more accessible caves. But you need a guide, flashlights or Petromax lamps to see your way through most of the caves.

Our first stop was the famous Tabon Cave itself, where the oldest traces so far of *Homo sapiens* in the Philippines were found. The cave, a large roomy chamber with a wide mouth, is located at the base of a towering cliff on the northeast corner of Lipuun Point. Inside, it is well-lit by natural light so that except to peer into cul-de-sacs (There's a hidden chamber called the "master's bedroom."), flashlights aren't necessary. The entrance faces the South China Sea, making us envious of the first tenants, who had a gorgeous view from their "terrace." The premier artifact of this prehistoric treasure trove is the skullcap of the 24,000-year-old Tabon Man. Although the artifacts have been removed, the excavations are still open and identified so we can see where each prized bone chip or shard was found.

The Manunggul Cave, tucked into the face of a sheer cliff 375 feet above the southern roof of Tabon, is as picturesque as it is perilous. It can only be reached from the side by passing through a gap in the cliff under an overhanging limestone bridge. Unless you're adept at rappelling or can swing from a treetop to the entrance àla Tarzan, be content with viewing the cave from ground level. The archaeologists had to build a special ladder to probe this cave.

As a burial site, Manunggul has no equal. True, the Ibaloi dead are as magnificently ensconced in the crannies of Mount Kabunian, but here, the resting ancients lie suspended between the sea and the sky.

Manunggul consists of four chambers with three openings, but only two were used for burials. The first chamber yielded the most significant artifacts—large, decorated jars, skulls and portions of painted human bones. Of these, the most outstanding piece is a burial jar with a lid featuring two souls seated on a boat sailing to the afterlife. The Neolithic vessel, now at the National Museum, is unrivaled in Southeast Asia.

Tadyaw, the largest burial cave in the complex, is a maze of tunnels connecting limestone cliffs and deep valleys. This cave once held more than 500 funerary jars. The floor is littered with pottery shards dating from 100 B.C. to 300 A.D. It is tempting to snitch a souvenir, but we manage to curb our acquisitive instincts.

Guri Cave is said to be the most attractive on Lipuun Point. Made up of numerous chambers and winding passageways at various levels, its walls drip with grotesque stone growths—fluted and fan-like stalactites and stalagmites and travertine terraces. These formations grow at the rate of one inch every 100 years. You can imagine how many centuries it took to create the cave, which, by the way, is a work in progress—the formations are still growing and changing. During the early post-Pleistocene period, Guri Cave was occupied by humans using blade tools. Today it is only occupied by fruit bats.

Sarang 1, the cave next to Guri, is breathtaking both for its antiquity and its sheer beauty. Its age was confirmed by a German exploring for petroleum who found a shell that was carbon-dated at 50 million years. It looks like a giant terrarium, with its roof serving as the lid enclosing a remarkable ecosystem of trees and shrubs that grow between the rocks on the cave's floor. Three natural openings let sunlight and rain in, keeping this "secret garden" perpetually lush.

If Sarang 1 is bright and enchanting, its sister cave, Sarang 2, is dark and forbidding—literally a black hole only bats have so far fathomed. We make our way through two of the chambers—those closest to the exit. But we have to give up. If you don't think a place can be malevolent, then try spending some time in Sarang 2.

BELOW GROUND, in Sabang, Palawan hides another natural jewel. Older guidebooks refer to it as St. Paul's Subterranean River National Park, although it is known today simply as the Underground River and is under the care of the local government of Puerto Princesa.

The road from Puerto Princesa to Sabang is a dust strip. Even the vegetation alongside the road is filmed with red clay. It is startling to see fishing boats in this arid terrain just as it is hard to imagine that less than a kilometer away, on the other side of the hills that line the road, lie the clear blue waters of the South China Sea.

On hand to meet us at the Underground River staging area is the supervisor of Puerto Princesa park, James Mendoza, a biologist turned environmentalist by avocation. Since he came on board, he and his crew have been preserving the area, cataloguing the wildlife and improving the site for tourism. He is briefing us on the Underground River, but our attention is pinned on something else. Mendoza is a big man, but he is dwarfed by an enormous *talisay* tree behind him, on whose reclining trunk grows yet another full-size tree—of a different species. A few feet from this arboreal wonder, wild monkeys and monitor lizards indulge the crowd, hoping to be indulged in return with picnic scraps. "Please don't feed the animals," Mendoza growls. "We give them enough food."

At the embarkation point for the river run, guides hand us hard hats and life jackets. The cave's roof sometimes drops to within a hairsbreadth of your head; as to the river's depth, no one has yet touched bottom. Each banca has a searchlight powered by a car battery and two boatmen. Traffic on the river is strictly controlled. Our trip covers only a portion of the 8.2-kilometer waterway, said to be the longest navigable underground river in the world, yet it takes more than an hour to complete.

Entering the cave's maw through a curtain of vegetation which separates the light from darkness, we say goodbye to the world as we know it and disappear into another dimension. There is no need to remain silent, but as people behave when confronted with the awesome, we are silenced by our subterranean surroundings.

The cave is enormous, the shapes otherworldly. Formed millions of years ago, the stalactites and stalagmites have carved a universe below the earth and populated it with visions seen only in dreams. The imagination teases the eye into seeing demons alongside angels in a Dantesque scenario of the divine and the damned. Sometimes we see a surreal playground worthy of a Dali where giant mushrooms and jellyfish mix with other forms for which we have no names. At times the cave walls sparkle as if they were strewn with diamonds, at other places they are inert and lifeless, just slabs of stones weary from carrying their bulk for centuries. Some of the limestone drippings bear down on us with their great weight, while others are as fragile as Belgian lace.

Only the bats and swallow swifts are real. Up in the crevices of the cave's roof, thousands of languorous insect-eating bats cling to their roost awaiting nightfall while the energetic swallows tear the cave like darts. The enclosed air echoes with the shrill cries of both species. The absence of light has robbed them of their sight. They must orient themselves by the sound they emit. Other animals have also adapted to this dark world. Beneath the waters, a group of Italian explorers have found eyeless shrimps and fish.

As we re-emerge into the light we see a group of bathers chasing each other on the riverbank. How delightfully boisterous they are. After being in a netherworld for what seemed like an eternity, this noisy, happy bunch is a gift of life.

A faraway nest

El Nido, Spanish for "nest," is a town, a resort and an expensive soup. It might also be a synonym for isolation.

Flying into El Nido and touching down on a dirt runway carved out of someone's pasture, you immediately feel the region's loneliness. Virtually cut off from the rest of Palawan, El Nido is surrounded on three sides by water: the Luzon Sea to the north, the China Sea to the east and the Sulu Sea to the west. Its only dry boundary is the municipality of Taytay on the south from which it is usually severed by an impassable road.

El Nido has a land area of 49,000 hectares splintered across a mini-archipelago with a population density of only 27 people per square kilometer. The islands comprising El Nido are miles from each other and the towns on these islands are set far apart. Even the 3,000 people who live in El Nido spend their days and nights alone on the waters fishing from small bancas or working modest family farms sparsely dotting the plains behind the soaring cliffs.

There are only two ways to reach El Nido from Manila. By private plane or public ferry. The airplane, which holds just 18 passengers, makes two round trips daily, moving tourists to and from the upscale resorts. The ancient and abused ferry, which runs every three days and looks like every trip will be its last, takes everybody and everything else.

El Nido has one of the strangest landscapes in the Philippines, distinguished by the omnipresent black cliffs, which are stark, unfathomable and look old as time. They stand in the sea, teetering on eroded bases that seem too fragile to support their massive weight, or rise out of the land, monstrous cathedrals overpowering everything else in sight.

We spent a week exploring the cliffs by banca and found no two alike. Not being geologists, we're not sure what they are made of. The chips lying on the beaches appear to be black marble. But the shape of the intact cliffs seems pyroclastic, thrown up from the sea floor by prehistoric volcanic eruptions.

Some cliffs contain large caves, which bear fanciful names inspired by their shapes, such as Cathedral Cave and Disco Cave. There are cliffs that are massive sheets of barren, inhospitable rock and others that look like hanging gardens, indifferent hosts to the *talisay* and yucca trees as well as to wild flowers such as begonias that cling tenuously to their sides. (At home we cajole our begonias with TLC and they won't budge. Here, exposed to the wind, sun, typhoons and with practically no soil, they bloom like crazy.)

In crannies and deep caves atop the cliffs, the swallow swifts make their nests, from which El Nido derives its name. The nests, which brought Chinese traders to these waters long before the Spanish, are the main ingredient for a gourmet soup cherished in Asia to this day.

Nest-gatherer Efren Repablo, 29, has been climbing El Nido's cliffs for the last 14 years. Although the rocks are as sharp as knives, he goes up without any protection. All he wears are a pair of shorts, rubber sandals and a gold crucifix wound tightly around his neck. Said he: "Climbers wear sandals because if they start to slip they can kick them off and grab on with their toes. The shorts are a safety feature too. Long pants can catch on a pinnacle and throw the climber off balance." The crucifix's function is quite obvious. While he seems rather blasé about his work, it is apparent from the nasty scars on his legs that these climbs are not, to say the least, risk-free.

The nests located on the cliffs of Big Lagoon on Miniloc Island belong to Elde Lagrada, also a climber. They were staked out years ago by his forefathers. Lagrada explains that nests are found by observing the swifts in flight and charting where they seem to land. There are about 265 registered sites, each containing about 20 nests.

Despite the dangers that nest-gatherers face—quite a number have fallen to their death—all they earn is P80 a gram. Dealers in El Nido sell the nests to restaurateurs for P200 a gram; the restaurants in Manila sell El Nido soup for about P5,000 a tureen. It seems everyone makes big money except the boy who goes up the cliff.

THE TOWN of El Nido, squeezed between a rock curtain and the sea, is a bustling community of working adults and hundreds upon hundreds of children. "It's as though the average age in town is 12 years old," said dive-shop owner Willy Amann, a German who has made El Nido his home. It is the ideal environment for children. The beach is only a few meters away, traffic is hardly a problem with only about two jeeps and three motorcycles plying the two dusty roads, and everybody knows everybody.

With the ringing of a rusty bell at 8 a.m., 775 of the town's children trudge off to El Nido's elementary school, a long low building divided into 14 classrooms opposite the municipal hall. They become the responsibility of Fe Gabo, the school principal. Kinetic energy wrapped in a blue uniform, she is constantly on the move, shuttling between her office and the classrooms. Born in El Nido, she received her professional training in Puerto Princesa. Asked why she isn't working in Cebu or Manila, she replied, "I am not unique. Many of our teachers, like Grade 1 teacher Genalyn Acosta, have returned after finishing college to serve their own town; in fact, many of the teachers here were my former students. Some, like newly arrived Grade 2 teacher Rosana Factor, whose family bought a farm just outside the *poblacion*, are here because they love this town and its people. Whether we were born here or moved here, this is now where we belong and where we are needed."

The men of El Nido fish. By 3 a.m. an armada of one- and two-man bancas, which were earlier littering the beach front, are now bobbing in the coves beneath the cliffs, searching for *lapu-lapu, tangingue* and *pating* (shark). By 8 a.m., just as Fe's school bell is ringing, they return, loaded with the day's catch. The *lapu-lapu* and *tangingue* will be sold as table food. The *pating* will be processed by Manila dealers into fishballs.

Alberto Rosasinia has been an El Nido fisherman since 1982. As he sat in his waterside nipa hut, amid fishing nets and lines which take up much of the available space, he talked about his work. "Unlike in Masbate where I come from, the catch here is good. The work is hard but we bring in about 30 to 40 kilos a day." As if to underscore Rosasinia's optimism, that morning a banca returned hidden beneath a giant manta. Their prize, so large it would feed 60 people, had to be cut up on the beach in order to be transported to the market.

EL NIDO natives Fe Gabo, Genalyn Acosta, and even our *bangkero*, Jaime Cordoba, never left for the big city, where there are more opportunities. Before we arrived here, we knew that El Nido meant "nest" and that the nest belonged to the swallow swift. But after a few days in town, the term took on a new meaning. El Nido is also a "people nest." In a country that seems to be in constant migration, what is it about El Nido that holds its natives and draws others from distant places? Perhaps what an old man told us is true. The cliffs are psychic magnets.

Half-buried on El Nido's beach are the remains of two large boats, the ribs bleached by the sun. The boats came from Vietnam in 1985. Was it the current that brought them here or was it the power of the rocks? Since the passengers had long been resettled elsewhere, we couldn't ask them. But every day we met store clerks, fishermen, innkeepers, who, regardless of their age, would eventually say the same thing: "El Nido is my home, I wouldn't live anywhere else." We ask them, "Have you been to other parts of the Philippines?" "Yes," they answered, "to study, to visit, to do business, even to marry." And then they return.

Perhaps the best examples of the ties between the people and the place can be found in two of El Nido's oldest living residents.

Tall, gaunt, his cheeks sunken and his fingers stained by years of smoking, Prospero Austria is a second-generation native. He has traveled throughout the Philippines and to the United States, where four of his nine children now live. Said he: "My children in America have been begging me to stay with them permanently. I'll be more comfortable there, they say. But I could never leave El Nido. My roots are here."

Sitting in his guest house/restaurant, the first one to open in El Nido, Austria reminisced: "My grandfather, a *barangay* chief, came to El Nido from Panay in 1885. He built the town wharf, which he later gave to the government. My father was a coconut farmer. When I was a boy, you could see clear to the beach from our house. But soon rows of new houses and stores started to rise across from us, blocking our view. Then in 1934 we had a big typhoon and the opposite side of our street was washed away. Come to think of it, so was this side. We got flattened. But we rebuilt. El Nido has been rebuilding and changing ever since."

Ellis Lim is another second-generation native. His grandfather came to El Nido from China. Born to a wealthy family, Lim was educated in Manila and could have settled there if he wanted to. "My parents made me choose between setting up a business there or in El Nido. I chose El Nido."

THE SEA is the lifeline of El Nido. It is the source of the town's livelihood, the principal "highway" system, and the venue for El Nido's most popular recreational sports. Exploring El Nido from beneath the sea is like flying over a silent world of forests, mountains and brightly-colored cities whose buildings turn out to be coral formations. Because the ban on dynamite and cyanide fishing is *strictly* enforced, most of El Nido's coral reefs are still alive and home to an aquarium of butterfly fish, parrot fish, moorish idols plus many others we couldn't name. Snorkeling in El Nido's shallower waters is often like swimming through a traffic jam. At one point we found ourselves pushing schools of fish out of the way to make any forward progress.

While not a Wonder of the World, the landscape is certainly a world wonder, making tourism the second largest industry in El Nido. Seeing Westerners in town is not unusual. There are several luxury resorts on the islands nearby and dozens of moderately priced pensions for divers in the town itself. Furthermore, to cash in on the tourist boom, it seems as though every home with an empty room is hanging up a "to let" shingle.

Tourist activities are planned around the landscape. On Miniloc Island we attended a musical evening unequaled anywhere we have ever been. The music was supplied by a trio (guitar, flute and oboe) from the University of Santo Tomas in Manila, the "auditorium" was the lagoon surrounded by cliffs. Our small boat drifted silently into the lagoon, which was only illuminated by torches and moonlight, when the air suddenly filled with the eerie strains of "Music of the Night." We were making the Phantom's entrance. Because of the strange acoustics created by the cliff walls, it was impossible to tell where the softly suffused sound was coming from until we saw the musician's barque. Plied with champagne, floating around the lagoon under the stars amid the sounds of Bach, Mozart and the gently rippling water, it was as romantic an evening as we could recall.

Less romantic, though equally unforgettable, was our day on a small island about half an hour away from Club Noah.

El Nido can be called either "Land of Nests" or "Land of Cliffs." But who would have considered "Land of the Lost?" Our adventure started as our group headed out by banca for Dilumacad Island, which, we were, told was a favorite spot for picnics and wedding ceremonies. They didn't tell us it was Jurassic Park.

We came well-provided with a hefty picnic lunch basket, and even a table and chairs, expecting to lunch in style. After setting up camp on the beach, we wandered further away to explore the island. Hours later, we returned to discover we had a visitor. The tables and chairs were overturned, our towels and bags were thrown around. Then we noticed that amid the debris were long, shallow dents in the soft, seamless sand. Tracks!

We followed them to where the sand was overrun by vegetation and there they were, not 10 feet away, three giant raptors. Well, actually *bayawaks*, a kind of local lizard, but they were large. Daddy lizard, mommy lizard and junior lizard were enjoying our hospitality and what was left of our lunch. They must have approved of Club Noah's picnic basket because they were not only eating the food, they were also eating the basket. And the napkins and the paper plates. Our guide reassured us that they wouldn't eat us. Still, meeting Godzilla and his family on this perfect primeval island was unnerving.

ALTHOUGH STRANGERS are more or less common in El Nido town, as you move farther away you discover how isolated this municipality really is. We were invited to a barrio called Barotuan, so remote the younger children had never seen an outsider, let alone someone with blond hair and light-colored eyes. Standing in small groups a "safe" distance away, giggling and daring each other to muster courage, one by one they came up to us and stared. We felt as though we were exhibits from Mars.

To reach Barotuan we left El Nido before dawn by speedboat. For the next one and a half hours we bounced over the crests of the cold choppy sea in semi-darkness. Suddenly the boatman turned down the engines and we idled through a fog bank, beyond which was the riverine village of Bukana (Tagalog for "entrance"). At dawn, hidden behind the low misty clouds that wander among the nipa huts, it looked like a still from *Apocalypse Now*. As the boat slowly moved up the twisting, narrow channel hemmed in by a tangle of mangroves, the powerful motor barely turning, you could imagine the "smell of napalm in the morning."

Barotuan is an inland plain (the first flat ground we had seen in days) scattered with farmhouses, rice fields and a church. The barrio celebrates three fiestas: the first in January to praise the Santo Niño; the second in March to honor St. Joseph, the town's patron saint; and the third in May to thank the patron saint of farmers, San Isidro de Labrador. We asked the town's 81-year-old founder, Joe de Guzman Jr., why they need three fiestas. He replied, "To show devotion". However, we think it was also to have additional holidays. Every so often farmers need to break out of a routine controlled by the agricultural cycle.

It being the third weekend of January it was the Feast of the Santo Niño and Ati-Atihan. It was more than a festival of devotion and joy; it was also a reaffirmation of their heritage.

Almost everyone in this town is descended from Aklanon migrants. Like their Panay brothers, whom they have never met, the Barotuans cover themselves in soot, don "tribal" costumes and carouse around the town square.

The celebration would have been lost forever had the village elders not made sure the younger generation, born far away from the mother province, were aware of their Aklanon traditions. Said De Guzman: "We will never let our children forget their roots."

So there we were celebrating Ati-Atihan among people for whom Aklan was just a word on a map and a place in their heart. The paths leading to the basketball court, which doubled as the main square, and the paths to the church were decorated with "Japanese lanterns" made from small inflated plastic shopping bags hung from strings. Groups of school-age merrymakers, sooted and dressed in homemade costumes of grass, grains and feathers, were mingling with their friends or practicing their dance steps. Meanwhile, the rest of the town crowded into the church, a converted granary with a broken corrugated roof.

"Palawan is my battlefront!" proclaimed Herminigildo Larong. Not an NPA guerrilla but a diocesan priest, he was talking about souls. "Because of the extreme isolation of these barrios, too many people have not received the Word."

The Word in Barotuan is delivered partly in Tagalog and partly in Aklanon. The service is a mixture too, and perhaps not quite the way they do it in Rome. While the barrio is nominally Catholic, the older animistic gods die hard in remote areas and worshippers bring roasted pigs, chickens, rice cakes, bananas and flowers as offerings. When the plate is passed, however, they also drop in several coins. It is their way of making sure all the gods are satisfied.

BAROTUAN MIGHT be a metaphor for all of El Nido: insular, elemental, rooted in the past, its very isolation protecting it from outside interference. For us, El Nido is the last outpost, the place where we have seen the end of a rainbow not 200 meters from our banca. It is also here that we met a people who are close to the soil and the sea, able to respect their environment as a feral ally and not treat it as some tame pet. But we are told about oil exploration and learn that the cliff we had just sailed past hides a drilling rig behind it. If oil in commercial quantities is found, what will become of Barotuan and Mr. Rosasinia's fishing grounds? Will a black-gold livelihood replace blue-water living?

Before we left, though, we talked to the mayor and he somehow assuaged our fears when he said: "El Nido is 67 miles from civilization." "Frankly," we replied, "we hope it remains so."

The towns of the Calamian

"Let's go to a leper colony." It did sound a bit far-fetched. But what we meant was Culion, which we heard was a picturesque island. It is part of Palawan, and we had yet to see anything that wasn't interesting in that startlingly beautiful archipelago.

There is a cruise ship, the MV *Lagoon Explorer*, that sails around the Calamian Islands and Culion is one of its stops. Within the week we were off, not only to Culion but to Coron, Maglalambay and Busuanga, Dibutonay, South Cay and Sico Cove.

The Calamian Island Group in Northern Palawan can best be described as an archipelago within an archipelago within an archipelago. This is no play on words. The area's 50-odd islands (many of them still unnamed) are a part of Palawan's 1,768 islands, which are in turn a part of the Philippines' 7,107 islands.

Calamian is known for its white-sand beaches, superb diving and the indigenous Calamian deer that gave the area its name. The deer don't seem to be there anymore but the beaches and the marine life can be found in abundance. In describing Calamian, underwater explorer Jacques Cousteau said, "I have not seen a more beautiful place in a long time." Photographer Paul Chesley selected the Calamian Islands for the National Geographic series, "Wild Shores of the World."

Our own enchantment began in Busuanga, Calamian's mainland, where our nine-seater Beechcraft landed. After literally bumping to a halt—the airstrip was a dirt road—we transferred to a jeepney and continued to bump some more across a meadow surrounded by mountains. We sort of expected to see herds of deer but found instead herds of Brahmin cattle standing motionless as statues.

At the port town of Coron, we got our first glimpse of our home for the next several days—the MS *Island Explorer*, a de luxe 80-foot catamaran.

Although Busuanga has the airfield, Coron is the "metropolis" of the Calamian.

There are two stories as to how Coron got its name. According to one version, a native of Cuyo, Don Nicolas Manlaue, christened the area Coron because its bay was shaped like an earthen pot. "*Coron*" in Cuyonin means "pot." The other version has it that Coron derives from "*corong*," the Tagbanua word for "enclosed," which is an equally apt description of the harbor. The Tagbanua were the first settlers of this municipality, one of only three in the entire Calamian, which comprises 50 islands, many of them still virgin territory.

The busiest part of Coron is the port, an enclave of piers abutting the waterfront and middle-class houses inland, each with a shingle announcing the owner's profession (i.e., Roberto Reyes, Ex-Judge, Ex-Fiscal, Attorney-at-Law, Notary Public). There are also restaurants, pensions, shops and a moviehouse called Vered. *Vered* is the Hebrew word for Rose, which is the name of the owner's wife. The building, circa 1945, is entirely made out of wood and bamboo. The facade, in keeping with its Hebrew name, is muraled with scenes from "The Ten Commandments." But, instead of using the Bible as his source of inspiration, the owner turned to Cecil B. DeMille. Thus in the center of main street is a two-dimensional Charlton Heston waving those stone tablets at a throng of painted "extras" wearing Edith Head biblical rags. It was as unexpected as seeing Coron's vice mayor tooling around town in a fuchsia sports car.

We discovered how "famous" the Vered is when months later, in Puerto Princesa, we were talking with an Israeli tourist about the most unusual sites he has ever seen. (Travelers always like to compare notes and top each other's stories.) "You won't believe this," he said, "but there is a moviehouse in a tiny town in Palawan called Vered. That's a Hebrew word." Yes, we believed it because we saw it too.

Coron is a commercial center and the port is alive with activity. Most of the fresh fish exported to Manila pass through Coron. It is also the principal market for the Calamian and the best buys are fish, of course, reed mats and cashew nuts.

AS SOON as everyone was on board the *Explorer*, the three-story ship left harbor. Our first "port of call" was a beach picnic on Dibutonay Island. Disembarking on the uninhabited islet, we chanced upon some fishermen returning to Coron with bancas full of the day's catch. They, too, were stopping for lunch and were quick to offer us cuttlefish and *samaral*, a delicacy that in Manila costs an arm and a leg. In exchange for their generosity, we shared with them our drinks and the chicken barbecue prepared by the ship's cook.

Our next stop on the cruise was Maglalambay. A fishing village wedged in between the hills and the sea, Maglalambay seems to have been all but forgotten by the rest of the world. However, there is nothing surprising about that. There are a number of forgotten towns in Palawan. Barotuan, near El Nido, is yet another—a totally self-contained island-barrio, so insular as to practically regard visitors as aliens from another galaxy.

Having no deep water port, the only access to Maglalambay was by the ship's outboard dinghy. As we pulled ashore, the entire town came out to say "hello." In this sense, Maglalambay must be a true democracy. When visiting small villages such as this one, we are usually introduced to the *barangay* captain or the local school principal who becomes our escort. This time we were taken over by everyone at once. "Come see this, come see that," they babbled at us. "This" and "that" was about the same as it usually is in small fishing villages—a great assortment of bancas heaped up with the nets, windlasses, fishing basins, anchors and the rest of the colorful paraphernalia of the sea—but we dutifully oohed and aahed. What was incredibly different about Maglalambay and which the villagers seemed blasé about, was the scenery. If you ever dreamed of visiting the quintessential fishing village, Maglalambay would be a *déjà vu.*

The next day we arrived in Culion. It was what we imagined it would be and more. We thought the town ought to be called Culion-Culion, because it was like seeing double. Culion was built as two towns: one on top of the hill for the leper colony and a duplicate town by the water for unafflicted family members and the colony staff.

Culion began as a fortified town founded by the Recollect Augustinians in 1746. Its four bastions are still up, and while they no longer serve as lookouts for seafaring marauders, they offer the best views of the surrounding islands, including Punto Higante, which resembles a sleeping giant.

The Americans took over Culion in 1902 and years later, in

1931, established a leper colony under the auspices of Gen. Leonard Wood, who was also a physician (although he is probably best remembered for the role he played in the pacification campaigns in Mindanao). A monument to Wood stands by the old gate that once separated the two towns. Culion was named a municipality in 1992, and while no longer a leper colony, it is still under the administration of the Department of Health.

Walking past the town square, the market and the parish church, we followed the dirt road up the hill and then walked past the town square, the market and the parish church, to reach an intact magnificent fortress church built by the Recollects.

If Culion is unusual, so is its parish priest. When we came to visit, it was Father John Chambers, who was born and raised in the Bronx, a borough of New York City, about 14,000 miles from his current assignment. Despite being a stranger in a strange land, we were sure he must have found one thing that was familiar: Culion is as isolated from mainstream Philippines as the Bronx is from the rest of America.

FRIENDSHIPS WERE easily formed aboard ships. We soon found ourselves in the company of a French couple from Strasbourg, Jean and Martine Sommer, who were visiting the Philippines for the first time. Armed with state-of-the-art everything to record their journey, they were lugging around 35mm cameras, video equipment and a tripod as well as bug spray, sun spray, nasal spray and tons of mineral water.

That night we urged a number of the other passengers, including Jean and Marie, to climb up to the ship's roofdeck to watch the stars. There were so many out that night it was like being in a planetarium. Although we're not astronomers, we have spent some time in planetariums and can identify most of the better known constellations. We feel that one of the most unforgivable things we've ever done was fall asleep in the Hong Kong planetarium (doing HK in three days leaves you exhausted) and missing a chance to futher explore the heavens.

We didn't want to repeat that mistake here. It was so easy to give in to slumber beneath the starry Culion sky, lulled as we were by the gentle sea and the cool breeze. To keep our eyes open, we fell into singing our repertoire of Broadway songs. Soon everyone on the roof was singing. None of us could carry a proper tune, but we didn't care who heard; we were singing to the universe, to something—or someone?—thousands of light years away.

The following morning, we and our other fellow revelers padded softly toward the breakfast table, extremely sensitive to comments about our "performance" last night. If someone so much as asked if we heard boisterous singing last night, we had a ready reply—we were serenading the stars. To our surprise, nobody said a word. Were our fellow passengers being polite or had they not heard us? Perhaps our voices were carried on a frequency inaudible to humans and our songs are still playing out there, borne by the speed of light, to extraterrestrial ears.

ONE MORNING we woke up in a white box. The sky, the water, the scenery all disappeared. The ship rolled and pitched; rain came down in sheets. We were in a squall, the prelude to a storm. Then as suddenly as it started, the white box opened up and we were once again surrounded by blue sky, calm water and, most wondrous of all, the cliffs of the Calamian at Sico Cove.

Our ship was dwarfed by black walls of giant rock formations rising out of the sea like a legion of shrouded monks wending their way up to an unholy cathedral. It was such a deliciously gothic place that we persuaded the captain to bring us ashore though he thought it was unwise because the weather could turn vicious again without warning.

It was worth the risk. Sico Cove's beach was pure white; with every step our feet sank into the soft sand. We parked ourselves by the trunk of a low-lying *talisay* and just stared at the immense beauty before us, trying to remember as best we could every detail for posterity: the rough, voluminous stone cliffs carved by the sea now still as glass; the fishing boat brought to shelter by the storm, its crew warming themselves over a bottle of cheap gin; the tiny crabs crawling sideways and leaving minute horizontal lines on the smooth beach; the wind roughing up the leaves of the *talisay* trees or teasing the sea, which retaliated by spitting foamy sprays.

THE CAPTAIN'S prediction about the weather came true, but we made it back to Coron before the storm broke into a full typhoon. We were supposed to fly out of Busuanga back to Manila the following morning, and we were grateful to wake up to a clear day. After breakfast we exchanged calling cards, said our thanks and farewells, and eased ourselves down the gangplank basking in the radiant light nature provides after a storm, as if to atone for its bad temper. But midway between the pier and the main road, a crewman motioned us back to the ship. He was breathless. The flight was canceled, he said, because two planes crashed. An overloaded commercial plane couldn't pull up fast enough to clear the mountain and an incoming piper cub crash-landed on the runway. It would take two days to reopen the airport.

We spent a good part of the day queuing up at RCPI to make long-distance calls. If nothing else, those fiber optics certainly placed Coron, Strasbourg and Manila in the same century. The Sommers weren't particularly impressed; they expected it. Trueblue Westerners, they have unswerving faith in the telephone system—theirs, of course. "So what's the big deal about calling Caloocan from Coron and getting through on the first try?" they asked. Innocence is bliss, we left it at that. After all, the Sommers would never have need to call a neighboring province, as we often do, and wait hours before they could get an operator who could make a connection that wasn't garbled.

When traveling in out-of-the-way places it helps if you have good luck, and upon returning to Coron we did. We ran into someone who was throwing a birthday party for his son and of course, we were invited. So were Jean, Marie and Raul Teehankee, our friend and photographer on this trip.

The birthday party was in a stilt house connected to land by a three-inch-wide catwalk (at least it seemed like three inches). We were thinking we might make it now in the daylight, sober, but what about tonight, in the dark, six or seven San Miguels later? But putting aside second thoughts, like the Flying Wallenda's we crossed the bridge.

In typical Filipino tradition, once inside the house, we instantly became part of the family—even though up until an hour ago, except for Raul and the Sommers, we didn't know a soul in Coron. Following our nose—the entire house smelled of good cooking—and making ourselves unabashedly at home, we went straight to the kitchen where the women were milling around an old woodstove, simmering pots of prawns, crabs and, to our delight, lobsters.

But the evening's revelation was *lampirong*. It was Raul who "discovered" it. Never a shy person, Raul poked around the kitchen to "inspect" what else was on the menu. There was this sack of something in a corner. "What's in there?" he asked our hostess. "That's ordinary shellfood, just for the household," she said, meaning it's common food, certainly not good enough for guests. "Can we see it?" Raul pushed. She dug into the sack and produced a pinkish shell as thin as *capiz*. "Can we taste it?" Raul pushed further. She put several pieces over charcoal. In a few minutes the shells popped and Raul did the first honor of tasting the meat. "Oh, my god," he cried. He was orgiastic. "Our turn," we said elbowing Raul aside. It was heaven, a cross between oyster and scallop. From there we couldn't be stopped until we emptied the sack. We also "attacked" the rest of the seafood in the best fashion, without spoon and fork. And to our surprise, the

Sommers dug right in with us, using their hands.

After dinner, everyone gathered in the living room, mostly around a pot of spicy *aso de leche*. As if born in Pampanga, there was Jean, seated on a low stool, fork in one hand and drink in the other, alternately picking at stewed dog's meat and taking a swig of beer while trying to follow a Tagalog song to the accompaniment of a guitar. He was thoroughly enjoying the company of what he called "the friendliest people I've ever met."

"Turn a bad thing into a good thing." With this Maoist thought we applied ourselves to very un-Maoist activities. While waiting for the flight home, we strolled around Coron, hibernated in its beerhouses on stilts, nibbling on *kinilaw* while gulping down gallons of San Miguel, blew our money on shells (we came home with a precious triton) and bought tons of cashew nuts. Meanwhile the Sommers discovered Emperador, which they thought was the best common brandy they ever tasted. They must have been serious because they bought a number of bottles to bring back to Strasbourg. Our only disppointment was not finding *lampirong*. The typhoon, according to the locals, marked the end of the bivalve's season. All good things must come to an end.

(Almost) Out of Africa

It is 5:30 a.m. Already up, the sun bears down on the clearing. As the morning fog lifts, the lumbering figures, mere silhouettes a while ago, now assume clearer forms. The giraffes are grazing, their necks craned toward the trees, their slender mouths nipping at leaves. They are aesthetic grazers: they have given the trees globular crowns that recall the artfully pruned foliage of a formal garden.

The zebras are out, too, trotting in a row, head to rear, like circus animals. As they move, their striped bodies create a kinetic canvas in black and white, Op Art on the go. Also on all fours are the elands, the impalas, the gazelles, the waterbucks and the topis, all grouped according to species. As expected, the secretive bushbucks are nowhere in sight. Highly territorial, they keep a tight lid on their whereabouts.

"I had a farm in Africa," the voice of Meryl Streep as Isak Dinesen play in our head as we watch this scene straight out of the Dark Continent. The impression holds until we rest our gaze upon the low hills surrounding the clearing. Up there, along a forest of *molave*, grow coconut trees rising to various heights as they follow the land's contour, which eventually slopes down to the sea. This is in fact the Philippines. More precisely, Calauit, an island in the Palawan archipelago, and a sanctuary of endangered African and native wildlife.

In Calauit's 37,000-odd hectares, African animals share sheltered space with rare Philippine fauna, including the Calamian deer, the Philippine mousedeer, the Palawan peacock pheasant and some 72 species of birds; in the surrounding waters live the giant clam, the sea turtle, the sea cow and hundreds of species of fish.

A WAR-TORN continent on the other side of the globe created Calauit. Prior to 1976, Calauit was just another viridian island on the northwestern tip of the Calamian Island Group.

That year, then President Ferdinand Marcos attended a meeting in Kenya where the International Union of Conservation of Nature (IUCN) appealed to the world's nations to help save Africa's animals from being caught in the crossfire and decimated by civil strife. Marcos ordered a search for a site in the Philippines which best resembled conditions in Kenya's Shimbu National Park. In August that same year Calauit Island was decreed a game preserve and wildlife sanctuary.

It was an auspicious choice. Calauit was not only able to do the IUCN a good turn, it was also able to help the Philippines solve some of its own environmental problems.

Calauit's vast spread of grassland, lush forests and mangroves and fertile waters offered a haven for a wide range of wildlife. But it needed protection. Its forests were being felled by illegal loggers; its animals were prey to poachers; its marine life was wasted by dynamite fishing.

In 1977 the animals from Africa started coming. The new arrivals were a feral lot. Even those of the same species attacked each other, having come from different herds. The climate upset them. Unaccustomed to typhoons, the animals were bewildered by lightning, thunder and strong rain. The heat and humidity exacerbated skin and respiratory ailments that they carried from Africa. Of the original 104 head, only 72 survived. In time, however, the survivors adapted to their new environment and increased their numbers prodigiously.

SPENDING THE night on Calauit Island meant living in Spartan conditions in the warden's house. It was a night of frugal meals, a hard bed, bathing with pail and *tabo* and doing battle with the most determined and gigantic mosquitoes one has ever seen. Electricity was shut off at 7 p.m., when one needs it most. After dark there's nothing to fall back on in Calauit except a good book. But how does one summon the sandman when nothing lies between one and the monitor lizards splayed across the bedroom walls except a preposterously thin mosquito net already sagging under its own weight? What if the suction cups on the soles of these nocturnal crawlers fail and they come tumbling down? And what about snakes? Some Calauit animals have been lost to their venomous bite or unrelenting grip. Why should humans be an exception?

Yet if one survives the night as we did, one wakes to a remarkable morning. At sunrise the giraffe Diego—trailed by his mate, Dodo, and their two offspring—nudges the warden's door with his snout. Time for our concentrates, he seems to remind his keeper.

The warden, bright as morning (he obviously wasn't bothered by monitor lizards or snakes), opens the door and thrusts out a hand cupping the nutritious granules into which Diego and brood proceed to dip their mouths, picking their way to the last tiny morsel. Diego then rewards the warden with a wet lick, delivered on the latter's palm by a generous tongue. The *en famille* exchange over, the warden and his crew hike over to fill the troughs with feed. As soon as the animals detect chow time, they gallop toward the troughs with alacrity and speed, the ground trembling beneath their hooves, as though the zoo let out.

This is just one of the many extraordinary rituals that have become routine on Calauit. The animals woo, mate and multiply. The leader of the herd, always jealously guarding territory, must fight the challenger to death or otherwise resign his claim. Only the law of nature rules the island. Which is how it must be.

VISAYAS

Being there

Ships are slow. They give you time to think. As the *Princess of Negros*, *Super Ferry 2*, and *Golden Odyssey* churn south through Philippine waters, we passengers wonder, what will happen two days from now when we arrive for the Philippines' most publicized party, the 50th Anniversary of the Leyte Gulf Landings? For those directly involved in planning the ceremonies, it is a question of everything working smoothly. The press is anxious about covering an event that will be spread across so many different venues. Returning American veterans are nursing mixed feelings over renewing old acquaintances and dredging up old memories, no doubt some of them painful.

What would happen next is beyond our control. Like the soldiers of the Pacific War who had gone to Leyte before us and who traveled on slow-moving boats as we are, all we can do is hope for the best.

While waiting to touch shore, everybody tries to make use of the time. Politicians pore over their speeches, photographers and video cameramen check their equipment and the Americans practice saying *matagal na tayong di nagkikita* (it's been a long time since we met). But mostly we wait. At night people talk too loud, drink too much, go to bed too late. And anticipate the morning as the constant vibrations of the turbine engines come up through the floor, measuring off the empty kilometers that are bringing Leyte closer.

Seated amid a throng of reporters, Jim Collough, 79, is waiting again. Fifty years ago he was with men his own age, from the 1st Cavalry Division, heading for something called White Beach. He found it at 10:40 a.m. on October 20, 1944, when, with adrenaline pumping, he raced ashore for cover. Tomorrow morning, at just about the same hour, Jim will head for White Beach again. This time though, instead of approaching by foot, the mayor will be sending a car.

Corporal Charles Martin, 24, of Echo Company, 2nd Brigade has already hit dozens of beaches, dozens of times. He is among the hundreds of marines who will take part in the two mock assaults, first on October 19 and again on October 20. His part in the reenactment will be over in seconds. But like the older marines he has never met, who sat in full battle gear 50 years ago and waited, Martin is waiting, too.

THE LATE October sun above Dulag scorches the black beach as well as anyone foolhardy enough to be walking on it. Yet today the sandy strip is packed. A sweat-stained crowd, about a kilometer long, lines the ebony shore, which for some strange reason known only to the military was designated "White Beach."

Throngs of elderly Filipino and American men wearing blue overseas caps are accompanied by elderly women wearing broad-brimmed hats made of reed; marines stand ramrod in full battle dress; photographers in bulky vests wrestle with their cameras. Meanwhile, local children in sandals and shorts dash about, oblivious to the heat.

Lance Corporal Brian Kisner, from Headquarters Company, 4th Marines, has been standing in approximately the same place for the past two hours. His assignment is beach security and he will be working on crowd control when the Dulag landing begins. Meanwhile he answers questions, poses for pictures and scans the picket line of ships on the horizon.

Finally there is movement offshore. Small dots appear beneath the lurking warships. In the next few moments these motes grow into LSTs heading for the beach. It seems like there are hundreds of them. At exactly 11:00 a.m. their doors drop down and hard men with rifles at the ready dash the last 10 feet onto the beach.

The Commemorative Landing at Dulag has begun. When Dulag Mayor Rodolfo J. Serrano was a boy, the arrival of the American forces was accompanied by explosions, fires and death. As he stands on the same beach today, all he hears are cheers. Fifty years ago the landing forces brought chocolates, cigarettes and the promise of liberation. Today they are bringing cases of bottled mineral water and the promise of a good show.

THE LANDING at Dulag is a smaller version of the rites that will be held the next day at Palo. The marines, now all ashore, are exhibiting the latest amphibious vehicles and practicing assault tactics. The veterans look on with amazement at how sophisticated military ordnance has become since they hit these beaches with their M-1 rifles. The children see the ordnance as still more toys to play with on this wondrous day. While tomorrow promises to be a ceremonial event filled with dignitaries and dignity, today is turning into a carnival. Some marines, still in assault clothes and camouflaged faces, improvise games for the children, using their hardware as props. The rest of the marines retire to the shade of a *cantina* to swap stories with the men who came here first.

Looking every inch the Tennessee mountain man that he is, Lance Corporal Peyton Ross is big, tough and ready for anything. But not today. Says he: "We were told there would be crowds watching, but I never expected this. They were cheering and applauding... it's like nothing I ever saw... I mean it's incredible..." Ross is tongue-tied, overwhelmed by the warmth of the reception and by the events of the moment.

But amid the fairway atmosphere, one remembers that there is also a somber reason why we are all here and this day closes on a solemn note. An LCU comes up to the shore and about 100 veterans, their families and the press board the vessel that will ferry them to the helicopter carrier USS Belleau Wood, where a memorial service will honor those who were lost in these waters.

The ceremony is held on the hangar deck, backdropped by the ship's enormous elevator framed by the sea. In moving speeches, Admiral Ronald J. Zlatoper, Commander of the US Pacific Fleet Area, and John H. Dalton, US Secretary of the Navy, go to great lengths to tell these aged warriors that they were heroes. But the men already know it. Three wear the Congressional Medal of Honor, some the Bronze Star, others know they are special by the very fact of their being here. A large wreath is laid down upon the water accompanied by a rifle salute. It marks the final resting place of fellow-heroes who couldn't make it here today.

THE 50TH Anniversary of the Leyte Gulf Landings at Palo on October 20 starts early but the sun arrived ahead of everyone else. By 6:30 a.m. the entire site is an inferno, though nobody seems to mind. The crowds have been here since 5 o'clock to stake out a good view. The sole recognition of the heat comes from bottles of mineral water the soldiers are dispensing; they seem to be worth more than gold this morning. Over by the press stand, a juice vender barely has time to place his carton of Tetra-paks on the ground before he is sold out.

At 8 o'clock President Ramos arrives to unveil the Monument to the Filipino Soldier, cast in the likeness of Rupert Kangleon, resistance leader and Leyte's native son. He will repeatedly perform unveiling ceremonies up and down the beach before he finally takes his place in the stands for the landing rites.

At midmorning the show begins. From strategically placed loudspeakers the familiar voice of local actor Bon Vibar booms out, "Ladies and Gentlemen...," as overhead a PAF trainer plane dressed up to resemble a Japanese Zero flies by, spewing a contrail of "deathly" smoke. On the beach a palm tree explodes followed by a series of explosions across the shores of "Red Beach." The LSTs land, the marines storm the beach and secure their positions. More vintage planes fly by, this time wearing the colors of the United States. At last, one lone LST begins its journey toward shore with its very special passengers.

Aboard that personnel carrier are Ken Metcalf as General Douglas MacArthur, Ernie Zarate as President Sergio Osmeña and Hernan Robles as Carlos Romulo—accompanied by their "staffs."

As the LST nears shore, "MacArthur" stands, waits for the ramp to drop and then takes the step that may very well become as famous as Neil Armstrong's first step on the moon (at least in the Philippines). As history comes full circle, albeit in reverse, this time it is "Romulo's" turn to ask "Where's Doug?"

A dripping wet "MacArthur" drawls over the loudspeakers: "People of the Philippines, I have returned..." and thousands of eyes mist over. For many in the crowd it is *déjà vu*. For the rest it is a national childhood memory.

That evening the crowds thin, but the ardor remains. The beer halls and the restaurants in Dulag and Palo are packed. At the commemoration site, rafts of oil lamps are towed out to sea as a final rite for the dead. But the fireworks and the crowning of Miss Liberation which follow are definitely for the living.

ON OCTOBER 21st veteran Jim Collough is making plans to return to Louisiana; Lance Corporal Ross prepares to ship out to a new base and another beach; the press corps is moving on to their next assignment.

Did the 50th Anniversary Celebration mean anything? For almost all who participated it was the chance of a lifetime. The young sailors and marines had an opportunity to participate in an event that was the embodiment of their military tradition and pride. Veterans were able to refurbish a memory that might have grown faint over the years. And for the Leyteños who lined the streets and the beaches, it gave them a chance to say "thank you" to their Filipino and American liberators.

Bohol in the rain

July to October are the wettest months in the Philippines—not the best time to travel around the archipelago. Nevertheless we decided to visit Bohol in September, begging the onslaught of a monsoon. It seemed like a foolish idea, but having seen so many sunny days on this Visayan island, we thought a typhoon would be a welcome change.

Bohol has all the clichés travel brochures too often make up to lure the tourist: pristine, white-sand beaches skimming the low-lying edges of the land; a pastoral terrain dotted with over a thousand otherworldly haycock hills in the interior central plains;

a sea that never wears the same color twice and whose submarine life puts on an even more dazzling livery. Even Bohol's stray details look like scenes usually reserved for souvenir postcards. The shell of a grand house built in 1825 looking out on a 16th century church; children playing in the surf; a boy, a heavy triton shell resting in his tiny hands, pressing upon tourists a souvenir from the sea; a woman napping on a church pew beside a painted wooden angel.

Now we would see how these fascinating scenarios would hold up during a storm. Would it all be washed away?

IT HAD been raining intermittently the morning we boarded the boat for our trip down Loboc River. From the road the boat looked like a riverside restaurant, complete with tables and chairs, a corner bar and a service counter. The spruced-up barge would lazily take us from the town of Loboc to the Clarin Bridge in Loay. Or so we thought.

The usually mild river originates in Batuan and passes through a series of narrow creeks that all converge in Loboc. From there it forms two arms: upstream it flows four kilometers northward to the Tontonan Falls, where a hydroelectric plant catches its waters; downstream it meanders 10 kilometers to Loay, where it empties into the Bohol Sea.

As the weather was turning inclement, the pilot decided to go downstream, following the current. We set off without incident, quietly savoring the lulling motion of the river as we were pushed through the gentle waters by the motorized banca behind the barge.

While it seems that any river in the Philippines that runs between two trees begs comparison with the river journey in *Apocalypse Now*, this one comes close. The boat chugged along the narrow winding banks, its sides brushing against the nipa palms and the leaves of acacia trees whose lower branches touch the waters. At other spots the river widened out into canyons to reveal a lush jungle of coconut trees, bamboos and *baletes*, hosts to gigantic staghorn ferns. Through the green curtain we could, at times, see spots of brown, the thatched roofs of houses peeping through the screen of leaves. We came upon two naked little girls, water nymphets to our eyes, bathing in the water. We encountered groups of women busily gossiping as they washed clothes, the sound of their happy chatter washed away by the higher-pitched laughter of children playing and the still higher pitched cry of the wild birds. Away from the riverbank an outraged human voice cracked at the air, a woman ranting at her carabao, gone off browsing somewhere.

Then suddenly, it became deadly still. A storm was on its way. The gentle drizzle became a wall of rain, our lazy cruise had turned into a race for the Clarin Bridge and safety. It became obvious when the skies opened and the wind roared that our chances of making it to the bridge, although we seemed close enough to count the rivets, was blown away. "We can't do it," the navigator said, "we'd get sucked into the open sea." Amid the now swirling water and blinding rain, the crew bravely wrestled with the unwieldy boat, polling it toward the bank. Two boatboys, still fully dressed, dove in to the maelstrom, ropes in hand, to lash the boat to the trunks of the nipa palms growing along the shore.

Although the boat was more or less secure, it still pitched and lunged in place. The winds increased to gale force, hurling the once inviting tables and chairs across the deck like unguided missiles. Using whatever weights we could lay our hands on, including our photographer's camera bag, we managed to hold down most of the furniture before they did real damage. We were in a full-blown typhoon and had no choice but to ride it out. It didn't help that our guide, Manny de Erio, had earlier told us the Loboc River was *nangunguha*, it summarily takes a human life every year. Two years ago we had been on a banca caught in a night squall between Batangas and Mindoro and managed to make it through. Would we be twice lucky?

Fortunately, before we were lost in contemplation of death by water, the storm ended as quickly as it began. As if someone had shut off a celestial faucet, the rain just stopped and the sun poked a luminous hole in the yet gray sky. Again the air was filled with nature's sounds. But the riverscape became something else. Under the pale light, shrouded in residual mist, the foliage glistened with an ethereal radiance. It was as if we were staring at an impressionist's canvas, at reflected reality. The river never looked like this on a perfect day.

We now had to decide whether to go on to Clarin, where our van was waiting, or to return to shelter in Loboc. The pilot chose Loboc.

THE RAIN we came to see kept us indoors. The better part of our days were spent in Bohol's churches, among the oldest and finest in the Philippines, and in Bohol's struggling museums.

It is interesting to speculate upon why the Spaniards chose to erect the first Catholic churches in Bohol and not in Homonhon off Samar or in Cebu, where they first set anchor in the Philippines. Perhaps, while they launched their mission of conversion with the baptism of Rajah Humabon and his wife in Homonhon, the island was too small to merit a huge church. Cebu, although bigger, was hostile. Mactan chieftain Lapulapu, who felled the conquista's leader Ferdinand Magellan, refused to pay tribute and accept the new religion, and certainly wouldn't allow strangers to build on his land. Bohol, on the other hand, was well populated. In 1879 Bacalayon, Bohol's first town, already had a population of 11,142. The natives were also friendly. The first significant event in the island's written history was the blood compact celebrated between Sikatuna and Miguel Lopez de Legazpi in 1563. (Ironically, its second historical milestone was the revolt led by Dagohoy against Spain in 1774, which lasted 85 years.)

While waiting for our driver to find us, umbrellas in hand, we started our tour of Loboc. Loboc has two landmarks standing side by side—one, a monument to man's folly, the other to the grandeur he can achieve. In the mid-80s, local officials had the bright idea of building a concrete bridge to span the Loboc River. This was to impress the Marcos administration in Manila known for its infrastructure mania. Despite warnings, construction was started across the street from the nearly 400-year-old Loboc Church. With every piling sunk, a piece of Loboc's heritage sank with it; the pilings were dislodging the church's foundation. As fate would have it, what the protests and warnings couldn't stop, history took care of. The EDSA Revolution toppled Marcos and with his dismissal went the Loboc Bridge, which now hangs midway across the river like a serpentine monster that has been stopped in its tracks.

What was saved is one of the most beautiful examples of colonial religious architecture in the Philippines. Loboc is a town of carvers and its church shows the hand of its talented sons. Massive in scale but delicate in design, its facade is embellished with cherubs and floral wreaths carved out of limestone. The filigree extends to the side and main altars, and in the latter is further enriched with hammered silver.

This grandeur is repeated throughout Bohol, in small towns like Baclayon, Dauis and Panglao.

The Baclayon Church was built in 1596. It is arguably the first stone church in the Philippines. San Agustin Church in Manila, a contender to the distinction, was founded much earlier in 1571. the original church, however, was built of nipa not stone; the present stone structure was started in 1586 and completed in 1606, by which time the Baclayon Church had already been up for 10 years.

While Baclayon Church is rather plain, its museum is stocked with religious and secular treasures.

Pedro Ugat, a retired teacher and Baclayon's volunteer curator since 1986, led us up to the inner sanctum of his realm, unlocking room after room of wonders. All we could do was gasp in awe. Here were images of every conceivable saint; librettos of church music printed in Latin on animal skins; gold monstrances, ciboria and chalices; the silver *anda* on which the La Purisima Concepcion, the church's patroness, is ensconced during procession; perforated ivory eggs from China once used for giving extreme unction; reliquaries, one of which supposedly contains a fragment of Saint Francis of Assisi's bone; ecclesiastical vestments trimmed with gold and silver, and so many more pieces locked away and collecting dust.

Manong Pedro, a veritable museum piece himself, annotated every relic with a mixture of pride and boredom of one who has been around antiquity far too long. "This tabernacle was carved by a Baclayon artist in 1600," he droned. "You can't find any other more intricate, even in Rome." The ivory Santo Niño from China is the only one of its kind anywhere, he noted, as he lifted the tiny image's smock to reveal its circumcised sex organ.

Everything in the museum is either on top of, or propped up in, utilitarian cabinets, much like dishes in a breakfront. There isn't any money for a proper display, *Manong* Pedro bemoaned. Already the original ivory head of the La Purisima Concepcion had been stolen. So was her necklace of Spanish coins. "I do what I can, but I don't have a regular staff or security. These treasures lasted intact for 400 years and withstood Japanese bombs, but they couldn't survive thieves."

Panglao, an island off the capital city of Tagbilaran, consists of two towns, Dauis and Panglao. Most of the folk engage in fishing or farming. A singular feature of Panglao are the thatched houses with bamboo whose slats are woven into diamond patterns. From afar they resemble oversize baskets. Towering over this unvariegated landscape are the churches of the island's two towns.

The church in Dauis (1863) is dedicated to the Virgin of the

Assumption, believed to possess miraculous powers. Legend has it that when Dauis was invaded by Moro pirates, the townsfolk locked themselves inside the church until they ran out of provisions and water. Suddenly a well appeared at the foot of the altar. It is still there, and the water remains remarkably sweet although the well is located just a few meters from the sea.

In addition to its folklore, the other interesting aspect of the church is its French cathedral windows. If they are a part of the original structure, they're as inexplicable as the well. Also to be noted are the bas-relief statues above the transept, actually a series of exquisitely rendered trompe l'oeil.

Panglao built not one but two stone churches, both from coral stones quarried from the surrounding coast and farther out in the water. The original church must have been burned or destroyed by an earthquake. Its ruins, an ornate facade, today serves as a shrine for the Lady of Fatima. The second church was completed only in 1924. As in Dauis Church, it is most memorable for its trompe l'oeil ceiling.

Like other old churches in the Philippines, wrote Nelson Navarro, Panglao Church has no record of the unsung folk who put this house of worship together—the able-bodied men who built it literally stone by stone or the women who sewed the ecclesiastical vestments and the rich robes of its pantheon of saints. As we also discovered, even the artist who created the ceiling frescoes, a life work and of a more recent vintage, had been forgotten. All the folk could tell us was that they were done by a former town mayor, "an old man wielding brushes, dipping these in cans of paint, and painting what the priest told him to."

AT LEAST at the Carlos P. Garcia Memorial Museum, the Boholanos are studiously reconstructing their past. Or trying their best. Like Baclayon's Pedro Ugat, Leonora Rama, the museum's assistant curator, is doing as much as she can with what little she has. Quartered in a house that belonged to the fourth president of the

Philippines, the museum contains Garcia's memorabilia and an eclectic assortment of artifacts dating from pre-Hispanic times to the Pacific War years.

The museum had just recently received a donation of old books, many containing etchings and illuminations. We were on hand as Mrs. Rama examined them for the first time. As she leafed through each volume we felt like archaeologists, uncovering old photographs, prayer cards, marginal notes and a lottery ticket left between the pages of the books, some of which were severely damaged by temperature, humidity and insects. It was troubling to know that even though they were now in the hands of the museum, there would still be no means of preserving them. The only thing Mrs. Rama could do would be to clean them and put them under glass.

What caught our eye was a reproduction of the Eskaya syllabary copied from a wooden tablet. Eskaya, believed to be Bohol's pre-Hispanic tongue, is now spoken only in the province's hinterlands. It has been supplanted by the more popular Cebuano and Boholano dialects. True or not, the Eskaya alphabet is said to contain borrowings from Greek and Latin. Scholars, however, are certain that it is the key to the Visayan languages.

Our photographer friend, Sonny Yabao, was in Bohol recently to shoot the island once more for a picture book. He came back to Manila full of stories. In Duero, a hill town, he met the Eskaya. "I took a portrait of this man wearing an extraordinary costume—a jacket made entirely of *buri*, the same material *buntal* hats are made of," he beamed. It was the first time he saw anything like this, and he has been roaming the archipelago for years.

His enthusiasm was infectious. We must go to Duero, we must see the Eskaya, we told ourselves. We just found another reason to return to Bohol, whatever the weather.

Dinagyang!

What do you say to a man wearing feathers, carrying a spear and dancing the Macarena? We don't know either, but there were at least 80 of them at the Freedom Grandstand in Iloilo City, participating in the annual Dinagyang.

Dinagyang, as it is currently celebrated in this premier Visayan city, is a little bit of religion, a little bit of folklore and a whole lot of Las Vegas. The intricate dances and ornate costumes are now closer to an MGM grand extravaganza than they are to the Ati celebration of King Marikudo's sale of Panay Island to the 10 Bornean *datus.*

The real estate deal, a golden *salakot* for an entire island-kingdom (probably rivaled only by the sale of Manhattan island for $24) is recorded in the *Maragtas,* a Visayan epic. It is retold and reenacted all over Panay on the third and fourth week of January. The central icon, Santo Niño, is a 16th-century adaptation that honors the first Catholic image to reach Philippine soil during the days of the Spanish conquista.

The Ilonggo version of the festival began 28 years ago as a small celebration to welcome to Iloilo a replica of the Santo Niño, a gift from Cebu City. In 1975, to promote tourism, the city gussied up the festival into something akin to the orgiastic Ati-Atihan (Aklan's number one tourist attraction) and added a Kasadyahan (Mardi Gras). The new festival included several nights of revelry, street dancing and food fairs. In 1977 a local broadcaster, in describing the now annual event, used the word *dinagyang* from the Ilonggo root word *dagyang* ("to make merry") and the festival's name was coined.

"It has become too commercial," detractors say. Maybe. But beneath the calculated glitter is the same psychic need served by every Philippine harvest festival: the urge to thank the gods for the season's bounty.

THE KASADYAHAN on Saturday and the Dinagyang on Sunday are held as "tribal" competitions. Each "tribe" consists of between 80 and 100 dancers and 40 drummers. Most of these tribesmen are drawn from the local schools. The themes of the contest are: Myths and Legends; Ilonggo Religious Rites; Ilonggo History; Fiestas and Festivals; Ilonggo Heroes; and Ilonggo Livelihood. The judging categories include originality of costume, choreography, overall performance and musicianship.

The judges for Dinagyang are a diverse group whose only

commonality is a familiarity with Filipino art and culture. Two judges while we were there, for example, were, three-time festival participants Frank Koopsman, a Dutchman and now a farmer in Iloilo, and Poli Abastillas, an Ilonggo fashion designer.

THE DINAGYANG spectacle is growing both in numbers of participants and in audience. Filipinos come from other parts of the country, and, more recently, visitors from Europe, Hawaii, Korea and Japan have attended. Harold and Beate Fritsch, from Munich, were quickly caught by the merrymaking. "We have street festivals back home," they said, "only not so large and not so noisy."

We arrived late for the city-wide party. All the Friday flights out of Manila were fully booked. If you are thinking of going to a Dinagyang you had better plan ahead. Planes and hotels fill up fast.

On Saturday at 10:00 a.m. the festival area was already packed with local revelers, tourists and "Stone Age" young men in loincloths and headdresses, bodies covered in soot imitating the Ati's dark skin. Their primitive appearance would have been more complete, though, if not for the occasional wristwatch and rubber shoes. (These were removed before performing.)

The parade portion of the Kasadyahan consisted of the various business organizations sponsoring the event. The amount of money needed to stage the pageant is far bigger than either the city or the provincial government can afford. The elaborate costumes alone can cost as much as P2,000 each. The remainder of the money comes from the private sector and NGOs. Many of these companies, as their floats passed by, showered the crowds with samples of their wares. Unfortunately the sponsoring banks didn't.

IF THE Freedom Grandstand was crowded Saturday, Sunday it was packed. Dignitaries and lesser lights shared common space in anticipation of the contest to come. After the loudspeaker garbled the rules, introduced those who thought they should be, and a child chosen to be the official Santo Niño was ensconced in his place of honor, the drums began to roll. One by one the tribes burst into the performance area.

Each group went through a series of dances from ethnic to break to ballet. Many brought their own props—lanterns, a replica of the Molo Church, even a Santo Niño of their own, although they couldn't fool us, since we saw the "real" one still sitting in his place of honor in the stands. Besides the "impostor" Santo Niño was a girl. If a saint might influence the judges, one tribe must have thought, perhaps something else would too—so they brought a beauty queen.

There were sights to see and sights that probably should have been left unseen. Tribu Bola-Bola, an ex-champion, kicked up dust with their sustained high energy level. They are a curious lot brandishing a *faux* ethnicity borrowed from the Fiji, Ifugao and T'boli. Tribu Sigabong dazzled the crowd with their seahorse costume made from *capiz* shells while Tribu Sagasa, in our book the most originally garbed, came as *pintados*, the essential Visayan. Tribu Himala's mouse-like headdresses made of rope were attraction enough, but the 80 tribesmen were upstaged by their mascot—a naked, sooted boy, no more than two years old, with "Bronx" painted on his forehead and "O-O" on his buns. There was more nakedness as a member of Tribu Matahari dropped his skirt in the frenzy, but went on performing, never missing a beat. The drum masters were a joy to watch as they jumped, clutched at the air, swung their bodies like gymnasts, all to draw out heat and rhythm from the drums. When the last tribe exited the performance area, the grounds were littered with the debris of celebration—a headdress here, a spear there, a scattering of pairless slippers, lost children still unclaimed.

It was a battle of the bands, a duel of the dancers, the competition as fierce as the competitors' make-up. The crowd took part too. Much like in a basketball game, everyone had their own favorites, and the cheering was almost as intense and incessant as the beating of the drums.

It was now in the hands of the judges and they wouldn't announce a decision for another six and a half hours. We didn't envy them. Every group was excellent and many deserved to win. If the choice came down to nuances, they were much too subtle for us. We therefore forgot the contest for a while and went exploring.

MIAGAO, ILOILO'S most famous church, has recently joined the UNESCO Heritage List. Built in 1787 by Fr. Francisco Gonzales, the massive yellow sandstone structure was damaged during the 1898 Revolution, again when a fire razed the building in 1910 and a third time in 1948 during an earthquake. Each time its most important architectural details survived, however, and the repeated restorations carefully preserved the folk-baroque character evident in the facade.

The pediment is dominated by the figure of Saint Christopher dressed like a native farmer, carrying the Santo Niño on his back while holding onto the trunk of a coconut tree. This central motif is flanked by indigenous flora.

The structure is also full of surprises in another sense. The 19th century inhabitants of Miagao sought refuge from pirate attacks in their fort-like church. Although it is now covered, you can still see the doorway to an escape tunnel leading out to the beach. We wondered, if the parishioners could get out, couldn't the pirates get in?

Having been through five hours of Dinagyang, we thought we were danced out. We were wrong. As we were admiring the church we heard a car siren and then a procession turned the corner. Suddenly the empty street was taken over by another Dinagyang, but this one distinctly homemade. It was about a dozen ragtag eight-year-old boys, with bodies blackened, sort of dancing in step to a Dixieland march band. Except the band wasn't marching. The musicians had crammed themselves and their instruments into a jeepney. The overloaded vehicle resembled a cross between Ati-Atihan and a circus clown car.

Trailing the nonmarching band were several floats on which pairs of boys and girls—who were the presiding royalty of this fiesta—dressed in their best party clothes. As the parade passed down the empty streets, the royal couples, looking like life-size wind-up dolls, waved to the non-existent crowds.

Jaro's Cathedral, regarded as the seat of Catholicism in Western Visayas, is also known as the Shrine of the Lady of the Candles. Her image rested for over a century in a modest niche above the main doors. In 1981 Pope John Paul II came to crown the image as Patroness of Western Visayas. When it was time to return the image to its niche, however, it wouldn't fit. The image had somehow grown larger. We first heard the story from our guide who grew up in Jaro and had seen the image in its original perch. At that time, he said, it was no more than three feet tall. "Really," was all we could say in the tone of the urban skeptic. But there it was. Looking at its former resting place and the statue as it is now, practically life-size, there was no question that something did happen. The image we saw couldn't possibly fit into the original niche.

AT SIX o'clock we returned to the Freedom Grandstand for the contest results. We were greeted by a crowd of thousands dancing between four massive theater speakers. The acoustic displacement of the air was actually palpable. We were literally pushing our way through a wall of sound.

The judges were ready to award six trophies and cash prizes to the best groups. It was serious business, as more than P65,000 was going to be distributed. And the winners? Tribu Atub-Atub, our favorite Macarena dancers, won for best costume and took second place overall. But it was Tribu Bola-bola, from Iloilo National High School, that swept the field in four special categories—performance, choreography, music, and discipline—and won P40,000 for placing first overall.

For the rest of Iloilo it was now dancing and drinking until the wee hours. For us and our hosts from the Iloilo Jaycees, it was a nightcap and to bed.

We were back in Manila by noon the following day. But even before leaving Iloilo we had made a vow. There is so much waiting for the traveler here—a friendly people, majestic churches, a substantial miracle, glorious scenery and a full slate of activities. We would be back.

Once upon a time in Malandog...

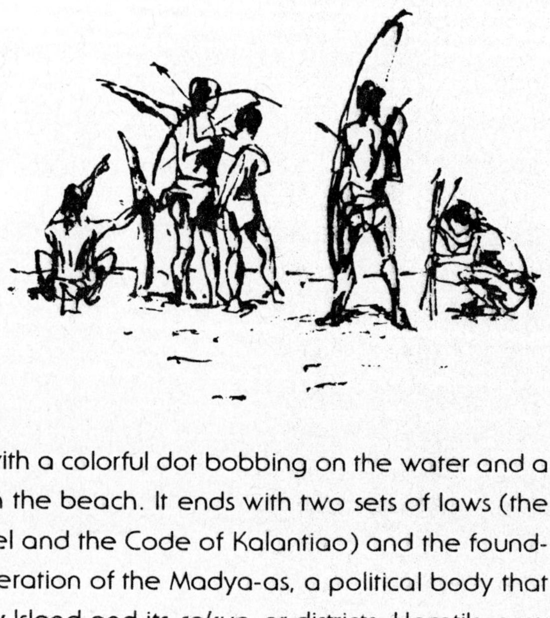

The tale starts with a colorful dot bobbing on the water and a group of Aetas on the beach. It ends with two sets of laws (the Code of Sumakwel and the Code of Kalantiao) and the founding of the Confederation of the Madya-as, a political body that is to govern Panay Island and its *sakup*, or districts: Hamtik, now Antique; Irong-Irong, now Iloilo; and Aklan, formerly Capiz and now divided into Capiz and Aklan. In between, the Visayan epic *Maragtas* relates a tale of discovery, mutual distrust followed by overtures of friendship, and eventually harmonious existence between two very different groups of people.

IN THE 13th century, to escape political oppression in their homeland, the 10 *datus* of the Kingdom of Bulunay (now Brunei) and their entourage, led by Datu Puti, sailed for greener pastures. Wind and tide brought their flotilla of sailors, merchants, carvers, farmers, craftsmen and *babaylans* (spiritual leaders) to Sinogbuhan, now San Joaquin, Iloilo. Unfortunately, Sinogbuhan fell below expectations, having little to offer in the way of food and fresh water. From there, Datu Puti sent one of his chief aides, Datu Sumakwel, to find a better place. Known for his obedience as well as his wisdom, Sumakwel took a similar entourage of wives, settlers, guards and his *babaylan* and sailed farther north to the Gulf of Panay, eventually setting anchor in Malandog, now a barangay of Hamtik, Antique.

An account of Sumakwel's arrival says, "*He surveyed the land [Malandog] and saw in his vision big harvests from the plain, much food from the rivers and the sea, and game from the nearby hills and mountains.*" He also encountered the original inhabitants, the lowland Aetas.

Rather than start a war with the Aetas over the island, the wise Sumakwel chose to bargain. Pledging to respect the lifestyle of the Aetas and offering them gifts—a golden *salakot* (hat), a golden necklace and a golden bowl—he won over the Aeta King, Marikudo. Eager to please their new friends, the guileless tribe surrendered the coastal land to the Malays and themselves retreated to the hills.

Sumakwel, an adept governor, ruled Malandog with an iron fist wrapped in a velvet glove. His laws were both practical and dark, and included such tenets as: Land should be cultivated and planted; the lazy would be punished. When a slave becomes industrious and an able worker, the purchase money should be returned to the purchaser and the slave shall be freed to till his own land. Poor persons should not have more than two children; the third child is to be killed and thrown into the river.

SUMAKWEL'S LANDING and the compact of friendship with the Aetas are the highlights of Binirayan, a festival reenacting the *Maragtas*. Begun in 1978 by Evelio B. Javier, Antique's most celebrated son, it enlists dozens of farmers, fisherfolk, shopkeepers and students—and the descendants of the original Aeta tribesmen to become actors for a day.

Says researcher Errol T. Santillan, who adapted the *Maragtas* for the pageant: "Each year we try to further involve the Aetas in this project. Originally we focused only on the landfall of the Bornean chieftains. Last year I revised the script to include a whole section on the Aeta culture prior to the landing I think it adds depth as well as historical accuracy to the story."

THE BASIC text of the *Maragtas* is celebrated across Panay. In Aklan it is the Ati-Atihan, in Iloilo, Dinagyang. Both are held in late January to coincide with the feast of the Santo Niño. In more laid-back Antique, where the festival is called Binirayan, Visayan for boat ride, it seems to move around a bit. For several years it was held in December. The year we were there it was celebrated from April 30 to May 3, which coincided with the feast days of San Jose de Buenavista, the patron saint of Antique's capital town, which bears his name.

BY EARLY morning of the reenactment day, the beach at Malandog was filling up. The entire town turned out, including the resident dogs. It was hot and getting hotter. Ice cream venders were making a killing. The air was filled with the sounds of ethnic music coming from two enormous loudspeakers, interrupted by announcements and the introduction of local celebrities. Festive tables were set up along the beach, laden with delicacies—roast pigs and cows, rice cakes, broiled fish, summer fruits, including the sugary native *sineguelas*. The food represented the Aeta's offerings, and after the pageant would be shared by all in a thanksgiving ritual.

After a wait, a group of Aetas in traditional tribal wear began to build a fishing village on the beach. We were amazed at how quickly a realistic encampment could be assembled. Some bamboo poles, banana leaves, a fire and you had a working Aeta community.

As the Aetas silently went through the motions of fishing, playing and cooking—the entire reenactment is a mime—the Bornean barge began moving toward the shore, bringing a riot of colors to the drab, leafless beach. Its red sail shone like a huge tongue of fire, its sides were festooned by bright ceremonial cloths. On the prow stood the *babaylan*, garbed in red, holding out a red cloth with which he searched the wind for the god Bulalakaw's omens. The loudspeakers switched from tribal music to the narrative, the audience pressed closer together to secure a better view.

As the pageant unfolded the role of the shaman became more intense. Probably a method actor, our *babaylan* literally threw himself into the part—jumping, chanting, dancing and waving his staff around. At one point he was required to bless the beach, an activity that had him running hither and yon in the midday sun. We wondered if he would survive the performance.

Mysteriously, previous actors who played the *babaylan* did not. They succumbed to a variety of illnesses within the same year they played the part. This year, we were told, the actor wore an amulet to protect himself from disembodied spirits.

The rest of the cast took their roles as seriously. And the story moved on with sincerity, if without polish, until the gifts were exchanged between the Malays and the Aetas and both camps, now in a partying mood, outdanced each other. Which brought us to a rather disquieting finale.

The sealing of the compact requires the ritual slaying of a wild pig, its blood collected in a cup. Up until now, everything was make-believe. The Borneans were Visayan farmers, fishermen and shopkeepers, the golden gifts, *papier mache*. The pig, however, was very real and very frightened. With good reason. Although its role was pivotal it would not be around to take a final bow. It would be dead (or almost dead; our *babaylan* was a better actor than he was a butcher). As we left the beach, we wondered whether this bit of gratuitous cruelty was necessary. Plaster of Paris and colored water would have made the same point.

HOW AUTHENTIC is the *Maragtas* and is it an epic at all? Scholars of Philippine literature claim that since the material isn't written in verse nor is it sung it can't be classified as an epic. Moreover, the recently translated account is more expository than narrative in form, another requirement of an epic in the classical sense.

Historians also find issue with the *Maragtas*. Early Philippine history has been mainly reconstructed from archaeological finds and on supposition. Whatever documents existed during the pre-Hispanic era were destroyed by the Spanish priests. The manuscript of the *Maragtas*, supposedly written in Sanskrit, would have been burned as the work of the devil.

And yet the material is of such importance to the nation's history that to clear the air a Maragtas Symposium was called by the National Historical Commission of the Philippines in 1968.

The *Maragtas*, says historian Gonzalo del Rosario, cannot be interpreted as "a starting point in the settling of Panay and the Central Philippines" because it came "too late in the Philippine Iron Age to have been a pioneering and colonizing event."

Other historians, however, accept the *Maragtas* for the purpose it serves. "The *Maragtas*," writes Carmen Guerrero Nakpil, "satisfies the Filipino yearning for a noble pre-Spanish past." Obviously, this is the argument Antiqueños support, the doubting Thomases be damned.

Fact or fiction, the *Maragtas* is a tale of Bornean voyagers who dared the seas in their quest for freedom. A topic close to the Filipino soul.

On safari in Negros

Preparations for the safari began in Manila. The original members of the group were Lyn Gamboa, president of the Negros Cultural Foundation, museologist Marian Roces and historian Enrico Azicate. They were conducting field research to trace the migration patterns in Negros Occidental for a new ethnographic museum in Bacolod, the first of its kind in the Philippines.

"Negros Occidental is a province of migrants," explains Lyn, who traces her roots to Tarlac. Adds Marian: "Usually when asked about the history of Negros, people just tend to rattle off the names of the two dozen first families and think they've answered the question. But we feel that's really just the tip of the iceberg. We want to go into the field, and through oral histories, language associations and artifacts, discover who the original Negrenses were and where they originated."

Since their itinerary would take them to a virtually unexplored Negros, far from the cosmopolitan cities of Bacolod and Silay, we asked to join them.

In Bacolod, our jump-off point, we had a foretaste of what the safari would be like. Literally. Our first stop was Bar 21, an elegant seafood restaurant. So, we figured, we were going to eat our way through the trip—a thoroughly delightful approach. After all, isn't food an integral part of history and culture? As a culinary expert says, paraphrasing an old saw, the shortest way to a people's past is through their stomach.

That night we feasted on *lampirong*, a delectable shellfish that recalls the combined taste of oysters and scallops which we first discovered in Coron, Palawan, and never thought we would savor again. In Coron we sat in the kitchen of a stilt-house by the sea gorging on the shellfish as quickly as it came out of the earthen grill. In Silay, although a uniformed waiter served it on fine china, we all still grabbed it as soon as the plate hit the table. As the stacks of empty shells grew higher and higher, Lyn mapped out our itinerary. On day one and two we would head south, day three and four, north. The details were lost on us because our brains were not as quick as our tongues.

The *lampirong* was only an appetizer. For dinner, we repaired to Aboy's Kamalig, a classic longshoreman's eating place—hard mud floor, no tablecloths, but excellent home-cooking in copious servings. There we sat side by side on long wooden benches with the Bacolod/Silay elite as well as artists, salesmen and cab drivers—all of us brought together by *kinilaw*, blackened blue marlin, *tanguigue* steaks, fresh crabs, *sisig* and so on.

Our first lesson in Negrense culture was well-taught that evening. Negrenses love to eat. This inclination, writes Silaynon Raul Locsin, has given his hometown the "reputation of squandering its fortunes on fattening the *pozo negro*."

LEAVING SILAY at six the following morning, we started our journey into Negros' past by heading for Valladolid, a 5th class seaside town with a population of about 30,000. Our first destination was, of course, a *carinderia* called Ven, where we had a full breakfast of *balinday* (another special shellfish), boiled and fried fish and thick native coffee that would put Manila's five-star restaurants to shame.

Having nourished the body, we went for a bit of soul. The church in Valladolid, built in 1863, was half up and half down. The newer portion, meaning renovated, was of little interest. Behind the new altar, however, were the ruins of the original church. A makeshift tin roof, held up by the original wooden posts, enclosed the ancient walls of the nave and altar. The floor, tiled with *terra fina*, was covered with guano, courtesy of thousands of bats that roost up above. Rays of harsh light filtered in through the empty windows and breaks in the wall, catching the dust motes in the air. The overall feeling was one of extreme antiquity.

Next to the church was a destroyed convent. All that was left were two walls enclosing a meditation garden. We decided that it would be the ideal location for an outdoor café.

ANCESTRAL HOMES are not limited to Silay and Bacolod; they are found all over the island. Across from the Valladolid Church and the town plaza, which holds a monument to Dr. Jose Rizal, circa 1896, stands the Ykalina house.

Trinidad Ykalina is 91 years old, her home more than a century older. The centerpiece, a Bogs & Voight piano built in 1929, she dismisses as "new." The really old baby grand was given away to a favorite niece. Her house, like most of the ancestral homes we were to visit, was filled with memorabilia: ivory heads and hands of *santos* stashed away in a steamer trunk; 19th century china; silverware and crystal in mint condition; a dining table that could sit—and once did—the *Who's Who* of Negros; and souvenirs from abroad whose bulk suggested pre-jet travel. From a wall crowded with family snapshots, she removed one taken in 1938 at a *bienvenida* at the Manila Hotel to welcome back a brother from his European tour. Without missing a beat she recited the full names of all the people in the group portrait.

Perhaps Trinidad, a spinster who lived alone except for a retinue of *hijadas*, was lonely for company. Or perhaps she missed the days when the big house played host to political meetings or musical soirées. She wouldn't let us go despite our repeated goodbyes. "Come back," she said. "I'll cook you rice cakes," she added, tempting us. "I make the best rice cake in Valladolid."

The women of *barangay* Tabao, another section of Valladolid, were occupied with something other than the need to entertain. Tabao is the weaving center of Negros, and every home seems to have a *sikad* (foot-pedaled) loom and a thread spinner.

"I learned weaving from my mother and grandmother," said Salome Guangco. Her family was originally from Tigbuan in Iloilo, a town known for its traditional weaving industry. Salome, like her ancestors, wove from memory. The *barangay's* signature pattern is a multicolored check similar to Madras. "This pattern is called 'Miss Philippines,'" said Salome, showing off a four-meter piece of cloth in bright red, yellow and green.

When not at their loom, the women knitted with homemade bamboo needles. Their creations, mostly skirts and tops, are marketed in Manila and sometimes overseas.

Beyond the roadside neighborhood, weaving gave way to fishing. Since it was mid-morning the boats were in and the fishermen were repairing their *pukot sa lasag*, a net used for catching crabs. Although they might not admit it, their activity looked like weaving to us.

We moved south to Hinigaran, another fishing town, where the main product is dried *tanguigue*. In stall after stall, venders hawked the "petrified" fish, which were strung in rows like fiesta buntings. A piece cost P100—not bad, said our guide Mai, for the delicacy.

If one buys the dried *tanguigue*, the next stop should be the town of Ponteverde, to buy *langgaw*, or vinegar, the dipping sauce for the fish. Not the commercial vinegar, *langgaw* is fermented from coconut sap. Facundo Millan, a retired school teacher who inherited the vinegar factory from his father, took us to the fermenting area, a small field filled with 300 hip-high *burnays* imported from Ilocos. "We used to deliver vinegar all over Negros," said Millan, pointing to the beat-up truck that had obviously seen better days. "Now the business is really just a hobby."

It was way past noon when we reached Himamaylan to share a picnic lunch with Mayor Menchit Bascon. Her table groaned under the weight of fresh shrimps, crabs and fish—proof that the town is indeed the fishing center of Southern Negros Occidental.

But Himamaylan made an impression quite apart from its riches from the sea. We noticed that all the buildings were relatively new, something we never see in these small towns. We were to learn that every structure in the town is post-1945. As the Japanese were advancing, the townsfolk decided that rather than give the Japanese sanctuary they would give them ashes instead. Himamaylan was burned to the ground. Along with their gutted homes went most of their past. They are still in the process of rebuilding, though things, they said, will never be the same again.

"Yes, we want tourists," declared Mayor Bascon as we stood beside a lovely harbor that could be developed into a seaside resort. "Unfortunately, we don't have the facilities yet, but we can arrange hosting in private homes if given advance notice through my office."

Tourism is the farthest thing from Mike Vargas' mind. "There are more urgent needs to attend to," says Ilog's vice mayor. One of the youngest elected officials in the Philippines, Mike serves the oldest town in Negros Occidental. Founded in the 1500s, Ilog was the first capital of the province and its premier trading center. It is so named because it sits on a river delta, one side facing the sea and the other hemmed in by the Ilog River.

The river is both a gift and a curse. It irrigates Ilog's sugar plantations, rice and corn fields and its estuaries are natural ponds for cultivating oysters, crabs and prawns. But it remains a wild force, periodically jumping its banks to swallow up the town, which is shrinking. The floods in 1969 destroyed half of Ilog, including the old church, which once boasted of having the largest bell in Negros.

Yet Ilog has managed to retain its charm. We drove inland to see the ruins of an old sugar plantation, the mill and the grand plantation house.

From Ilog it is possible to drive back to Bacolod in about three hours but we opted to spend the night in a small pension in Kabankalan just 10 minutes from the new Ilog municipal building. The pension was modest and at best serviceable. Mostly it saved our driver several extra hours on the road.

The next day, we returned to Ilog to visit its caves. The trail to the caves, which are located in barrio Dancalan, is a narrow path between two mountain walls. Alongside the path there is a shallow stream which we had to cross now and again. Despite our having to remove our shoes and roll up our pants frequently, it was an easy walk, except for the steamy jungle heat. The ground was hot, the air was hot, the rocks and roots we clung to for support were hot. Not even the worst summer days in Manila come close. It was a unique experience. All we could compare it to was walking through a vast sauna to which someone added the pungent aroma of decaying vegetation.

Dancalan has four caves: Cueva Tubig, a water cave; Cueva Kabog, or bat cave; Cueva Sayaw, where the folk say the bats seem to dance as they dart around the cave walls; and Cueva Insik, a cave owned by a Chinese who mines phosphates there.

Returning muddy, sweaty and stinky, we were ill at ease with ourselves—especially since our next stop was the palatial home of Juan Jose and Paloma Vidaurrazaga at Hacienda San Isidro.

It was hard to believe that this substantial villa was part of Ilog. Or perhaps our disbelief could be blamed on our middle-class minds. Sure we had heard how *hacenderos* lived, how their estates were also pleasure palaces installed with swimming pools, gymnasiums, bowling alleys and riding stables. But seeing it was something else.

Juan Jose, a Basque conceived in the Philippines, born in Spain, educated in Europe and transplanted back to the Philippines, is a third-generation Negros *hacendero*. He was responsible for building Hacienda San Isidro into what it is today—a vast tract of sugarcane fields whose size is beyond the imagination's grasp. "He still attends to the *hacienda*'s day-to-day activities, though much of the work has been relegated to our son," explains his wife.

Yet what was most impressive about Vidaurrazaga wasn't his money but his mind. His house is filled with books, including a sizable collection of Filipiniana and historical arcana that even the University of the Philippines or Ateneo de Manila University do not have on their hallowed shelves. "I could stay here forever," said Enrico, our historian companion. So could we. Because apart from the books there was a remarkable collection of video tapes, among them classic films, BBC productions, ballets and operas.

DAY THREE was long and hectic. Starting from Silay before sun-up, we traveled north, then east and finally south, skimming through the scenic coastal towns of Victorias, Cadiz, Escalante, Calatrava and San Carlos, finally crossing the boundary into Negros Oriental to reach Kanlaon City.

Kanlaon City lies at the foot of Mount Kanlaon, the highest

peak in Central Philippines. Rising 2,645 meters, the volcano has two craters. The locals believe it is a sacred volcano, the dwelling place of spirits.

There are various versions on how the mountain was named. We found a rare source, the city's Historical Data Paper, published in 1955, which contained stories of Kanlaon's origins when it was still a town. One legend has it that Prince Kan and Princess Laon fell in love over their parents' objections. They eloped into the woods, where they were followed and killed. Their bodies were put in a common grave that grew and grew until it became a volcano. Hence the name of the mountain. Another legend is filled with historical license. Kan, the woman who lived in the mountain, had two suitors, one Sumatran, the other Indian. She spurned both. Thus her abode was referred to as being the property of "*Kan nga laon,*" or "Kan the spinster."

Mount Kanlaon may be approached from two different directions. One is through Mambucal, which leads to Mount Kanlaon National Park, a 25,000-hectare wilderness. Rare indigenous species, such as the bleeding heart Pigeon and the Negros fruit dove, are protected in this park, which makes bird-watching a prime attraction. The other way is through Kanlaon City. The lookout point on the mountain slope offers a commanding view of Sipaway Island, also known as Refugio Island, astride Tanon Strait, the sealane of migrating dolphins and whales. We could only imagine pods of these great creatures swimming by, but the lonely crow flying overhead and the swarm of dragonflies dancing around us were for real.

Our host in Kanlaon City was a feisty lady, Natividad Bautista, who, with her late husband, Isidro Bautista, founded the town in 1946. It became a city in 1967. "I gave Kanlaon its name, in honor of the mountain," she recalled with pride. "I also chose Saint Joseph as the town's patron saint, because we got married on his feast day."

Isidro Bautista served as Kanlaon's mayor for three terms,

mostly doing pioneering work. Today Kanlaon City is known as the vegetable garden of Negros.

Natividad Bautista, now in her late 80s, is a living treasure. Still ever the pioneer, practically everything she needs she grows on her own farm and backyard. In her tidy bungalow, the air smells of pine and the grounds are laden with trees dripping with fruit. She makes her own jam from *bignay* berries, bottles *santol* preserves and at one time, before the war, cultivated silk-worms and wove silk. "When I was younger, I rode horses, went hunting in the forest, I did what any man could do." And perhaps more. She also raised eight children, now all professionals and some living abroad. None of them live with her now. "That's how I want it," she says. "I raised my children to become independent adults."

We wanted to linger, to sit at her feet and listen to her stories about the Revolution, about Aguinaldo who was a guest at her house, about Quezon who dropped by on his way to Australia. But the clock was ticking away, it was time to go. The drive back to Silay was a good four hours and we wanted to see what Kanlaon looked like from the lowlands when it was bathed in the waning afternoon light.

MINDANAO

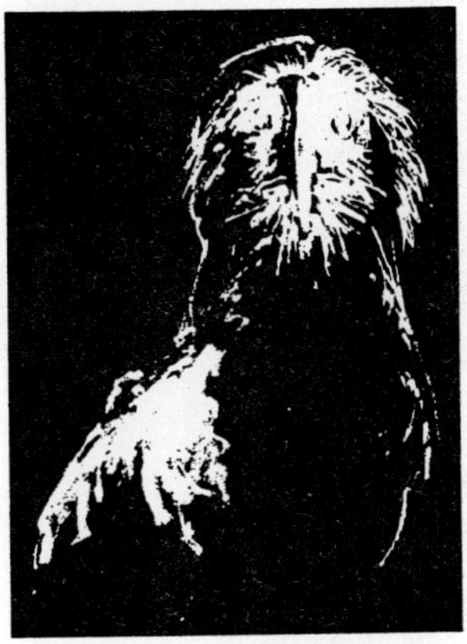

Under the volcano

Like spinach served on bone china.

That was our first impression of Camiguin Island as we saw it from the "ro-ro" (roll in, roll out) boat. The roundish island that lay before us was gilded with white, translucent sand which sloped upwards into a rain forest.

SOMEWHERE IN Camiguin there must be an old soul who remembers, from stories handed down by his ancients, how the island was formed. Unfortunately, our four-day stay on the island was too short to look for this living treasure. What we did find were scientific treatises supplied by the local Phivolcs (Philippine Institute of Volcanology and Seismology) which read like folklore. It seems whether it's recorded in molecules or myth, all creation stories recall the same romantic tales.

Camiguin lies off Cagayan de Oro City. It is separated from the northern coast of Mindanao by Gingoog Bay and Macajalar Bay, and from Bohol by the Mindanao Sea. Forged by fire and water, it sprang from the bowels of the ocean after a series of prehistoric volcanic eruptions. Still inchoate, the island, which is named after the Camiguin Tanda Volcano, continued to grow by accumulating layer upon layer of lava.

In time, volcanic peaks appeared on its southeastern slopes: Guinsiliban, whose explosions were short-lived; Mount Uhay, whose vent and craters were more active; and Mount Mambajao, which reached its present height of 1,525 meters through continual dome-building.

From its fiery formation, Camiguin, no bigger than 300 square kilometers, is like no other place on earth, ringed by seven volcanoes and countless crater domes. Of its volcanic peaks, only Hibok-Hibok remains active and is said to erupt every 35 years. "Its last eruption was in 1951, killing over 2,000 people," islanders say. "The next one is seven years overdue," they add with nervous laugh.

Surprisingly, despite the island's chaotic birth, there is little hint of a dangerous life under the volcano. Nature, as if making up for its bad temper, has swept away the reminders of past volcanic eruptions: the ruins of a half-buried church are covered with vines and a wasted cemetery has been claimed by the sea. With cinder and ash tucked beneath lush vegetation, Camiguin seems to leap out from the pages of a glossy picture book—a small island of small towns lying under a tropical jungle, all never too far away from the sea.

CAMIGUIN WAS once a part of the vast empire of Sultan Dipatuan Kudarat, the powerful ruler of Mindanao and Sulu during the 17th century. Guinsiliban was its first known settlement and its original inhabitants, the Manobo, retreated to the hinterlands of Mindanao when the Visayans came. Ferdinand Magellan dropped by Camiguin in 1521, before he made his historic landing in Cebu. Formerly a part of Misamis Oriental, Camiguin became a separate province in 1968.

Don Vicente Elio y Sanchez, an alumnus of Ateneo and a contemporary of Dr. Jose Rizal, kept a journal of his stay in Camiguin more than a century ago:

> Good bridle paths connected the towns, except during the rainy season which render them impassable... The streets are few, short, tortuous and hazardous... But from Agojo to Mambajao, the road is always good and coaches can travel on it.
>
> Mambajao is the most cosmopolitan town in the island, for besides the Boholanos and Camigueños, there are Spaniards, Tagalogs, Cebuanos, Leyteños, Cagayanos, Surigaonons, Ilocanos, Pangasinenses, Panayons and the indispensable Chinese, so that our neighbors call this town the New York of Mindanao.
> The view the town presents from the sea is beautiful, resembling a *crib* or belen, since, as a result of the rough terrain, houses appear one on top of the other.
>
> The town is completely provided for [in the way of] sustenance as well as luxury. Neither goods of the country nor the best of Europe that arrive in Manila are scarce here. There is fresh meat daily, for cows are slaughtered every day... Pigs fall under the cutting edge of the bolo, four or five times daily. Fresh and dried fish are always available. There is sufficiency of chicken, sheep, goats, turkeys and doves... For the common good, some rich residents have financed the construction of a system of bamboo pipes to carry water to the residential area of the town... Regarding cloth and other items... the town is well provided for in the

16 to 20 stores owned by Spaniards, natives and Chinese. There is also a public clinic with a full-time physician... There are three public billiard halls for enjoyment and recreation."

DON VICENTE might as well be talking about Camiguin today. The island is little changed. Primarily, the number of "souls" on the island, as he called his demographic count of 26,381 inhabitants, has more than doubled. And while one can never mistake Mambajao for New York, the island's capital town is still very much a melting pot and has added the Ifugao to Don Vicente's list of immigrants.

As for Mambajao's cosmopolitan air, the town does try to keep up with the trappings of urban life. Among the young, grunge is in style, at least the costume if not the attitude; kids here may be hip but are never sassy.

Life is taken one day at a time. Near the center of town we ran into a Westerner (he turned out to be Australian) tinkering with a motorcycle. We asked him what he was doing here. He pointed to a kiosk selling souvenir trinkets and said it was his. "But there aren't any tourists here," we said. "I guess that's why business has been off," he replied, contentedly returning to his motorcycle.

There are no moviehouses in Mambajao—or anywhere else on the island—but some savvy entrepreneurs who own videotape machines or laser disc players turned their parlors into public video rooms, where for P10 one can watch a double program. Movie magazines proliferate and Brandon Lee's latest derring-do as well as Sharon Cuneta's current state of lovelessness are very much the topics of Mambajao small talk.

In addition to Don Vicente's billiard halls, the prime forms of entertainment are discos, beerhouses and, during the fiesta month of November, the *feria* (carnival). In the shops one can find everything, from Black Label to *piñato*, a chewy candy made from peanut and honey.

Mambajao's picturesqueness, which Don Vicente singled out, continues to be there for today's visitor, especially in the early morning when the mist rolls up like a theater curtain and reveals the town little by little: first, the shoreline and low-lying edges of the beaches and then the fields, neighborhoods and trees and finally, Mounts Mambajao and Hibok-Hibok in their full glory.

In addition to Mambajao, Camiguin is made up of four other towns: Mahinog, Catarman, Sagay and Guinsiliban, each as charming as the other. There are two islets, Mangigue and White Island, both a short boatride from the mainland.

A 64-kilometer road encircles the island, which, as Don Vicente had earlier described it, is still better negotiated on horseback or on foot. It takes about three hours to drive around it. But we chose to do the island bit by bit, letting it come to us at its own pace. We arrived on a Tuesday but it felt like a Sunday. As the week wore on, the days completely lost their character. A day would be remembered as the day at the falls or at the beach or the day we dined with two mountain climbers.

THE FIRST town we saw was Guinsiliban, where the "ro-ro" docked. It was a welcome sight, a piece of country lined with bamboo houses jutting out over the sea and wreathed with bougainvillea. We had been sailing for three hours and although the sea was calm, our boat pitched and lunged. It was just too old to make the journey; not even a fresh coat of blue paint could hide its age.

At Ardent Hot Spring, our base, we "took the waters." The resort is located at the base of Mt. Hibok-Hibok in Tagdo, Mambajao, the source of the hot springs. Rainwater passes through the volcano's lava bed before it flows out to a natural catch basin at the volcano's foot.

The water in the thermal pools dotting Camiguin averages 50 °C when it comes out from the volcanic vents and cools down to around 30°C by the time it reaches the bathing areas. All over the island these pools flow freely, ceaselessly, gallon upon gallon.

Will it ever cool down or dry up? "Not in a thousand years," we are told, "which is how long it takes for a slab of lava, the size of a dining room table, to lose its heat completely. As for drying up, that will happen only if it stops raining in Camiguin, an unlikely event since it rains almost every afternoon."

Right behind the resort is a footpath to Hibok-Hibok, making Ardent the starting point for climbers opting for an easy conquest of the volcano. Joseph Omnes and Venus Guadalope, two climbers, were resting outside their pup tent when we stumbled on them. Their gear—hefty backpacks, sleeping bags, portable stove, hiking boots, thermal clothes, gadgets hung on their belts—indicated they were no amateurs. So why did they take the "baby" route up?

"This is our fifth mountain," said Venus. She and Joseph had already conquered the difficult mountains of Mindanao, including Mt. Apo, the highest Philippine peak. The 1,250-meter Hibok-Hibok, approached from Ardent, was like a walk in the park. "We've climbed Hibok-Hibok before, starting from Sagay on the northeastern side, across the Tuasan Falls. That's the hard way. But we just had to climb it again. It's so lovely up there, so peaceful—just us, the rolling fog, the jagged crests of other mountains and a full view of White Island.

OUR PUMP boat for White Island pushed off from Agoho, where the sand was black and the sea a deep blue. Then after 300 yards, the water turned green. The color line dividing the sea was distinct, as deliberate as the floating buoys that cordoned off the beach's swimming area. The closer we got to White Island, the lighter the sea color became. It was as if we were traversing a color chart, moving from one hue to the next, from emerald to aqua to almost white.

Landing on White Island, we had to protect our eyes as the

bright sunlight bouncing off the soft white sand rendered almost everything invisible. Across the empty sandbar the only spot of color was two black smudges—the sunburned bodies of Caucasian tourists lying on the soft sand. Later another boatload of tourists arrived, but they huddled under the shade of beach umbrellas.

"White Island is about a kilometer long," our guide informs us. "But that's not really accurate, its size changes with the tide." A movable island. A living island. We felt as if we were riding on the back of an enormous, white-skinned sea creature.

"*HIMIGO, HIMIGO!*" cried a child as we got out of our jeep in Mambajao. Jaime Go? Was he telling us his name or calling out to someone else? But he was talking to us even as he hid behind his mother's skirt.

It was only much later after we heard "*Himigo, Himigo*" again and again, that we were able to make out what the child was trying to say. In a town where everybody knows everybody, the stranger is easy to spot. And a citified Filipina, an American and a photographer weighed down with equipment made our party stand out like a trio from Planet X. So everywhere we went, we were greeted with a cheery "*Hi, Amigo,*" the standard salutation from native to outsider. We were sorry we didn't return the child's greetings. He had undoubtedly been trained early in the ways of what is probably the friendliest island in the country.

Writer Nestor Torre, who hails from Cagayan de Oro City and is a constant visitor of Camiguin, is awed by the island folk's unquestioning trust in people. "On my first visit, I was deeply moved when I found out that many residents didn't bother to lock their doors at night," he writes. "On a more recent visit, however, I was saddened to see that Camigueños now barred their homes." Has crime come to Camiguin? We don't think so. We would like to think it's because an aggressive lock salesman came to town and the people were just too polite to say no.

A city in search of itself

Davao City is hard to pin down. It is easy to put a finger on other far-flung Philippine cities like Vigan and Cebu. One look at these places and wham! instant recognition. They engrave their features in your mind as indelibly as genetic imprinting. Not so with Davao. It has too many parts to fall within easy classification.

Exploration of what is now Davao started in 1528 when a Spanish fleet visited the Sarangani Islands, which lie at the southwestern entrance of the Davao Gulf. In 1543 another expedition explored the shoreline of what is now Davao Oriental. Almost another 50 years passed, however, before the Spaniards established the first permanent settlement in Davao at Caraga. Spanish political control over the Muslim area didn't occur until 1848, under the leadership of Don Jose Oyanguren.

TODAY'S DAVAO City, measuring 224,000 hectares, is reputedly the biggest city in the world in land area. You can drive nonstop at 100 kmph for two hours in one direction and still be within the city limits.

It is also said that good fortune seems to smile on the Davao provinces. Because they are located outside the typhoon belt, the climate is moderate year-round and the soil, perpetually fertile. Since Davao, called the nation's last frontier, was opened to pioneers during the postwar years, the promise of its riches attracted homesteaders from all over the Philippines.

And so Davao City has many faces.

One portion of Davao is an urban enclave subject to the ups and downs of average city life. First-time visitors often get the impression that this is the length and breadth of the city. Call it the city proper then. But it is in itself an area carved up into differentiated districts occupied by government, business, trade, communications, 18 colleges and two universities, the upscale communities of the city's "instant millionaires" and the working-class ghettoes, which in Isla Verde is an aging, if still picturesque, village on stilts.

However, it is a face of Davao that bears little resemblance to the rest of the city. Outside of the metropolis, the terrain rambles farther than the eye can see into hundred-year-old hardwood forests and the newly developed commercial orchards.

This Davao is a fruit bowl and a flower bed. In terraced gardens Davaoeños are able to grow a profusion of orchids, among them the *Vanda sanderiana*, or *waling-waling*, one of the showiest orchid species in the world. (It is said that a German botanist found the mother plant growing wild on the slopes of Mount Apo.)

Davao's rich agricultural lands are seeded with all kinds of export quality fruits like bananas, mangosteen, pomelo, *lanzones, rambutan* and, of course, the *durian*. The road to Calinan passes through the fruit-growing districts, where vast plantations, usually citrus, are found. In the northern valleys they grow the famous Cavendish bananas, 90 percent of which are exported to Japan and other Asian countries.

But the best place for a visitor to try the fruits of Davao is the Madrazo Fruit Center right in the heart of the city. From September to November a cornucopial selection awaits you. Not only are the fruits freshly picked, they cost a quarter of what you would pay for them in Manila.

Davao is also a sanctuary. On the slopes of Mount Apo, the king of Philippine mountains, nests the majestic Philippine eagle. In addition, the nature conservatory in Malagos is also home to a wide variety of indigenous flora and fauna.

Another Davao is an aquarium. The sea yields up tons of fish which are unloaded at the city wharf every day. (If a Sunday fisherman in Davao says that he let a marlin THIS BIG get away, you can be sure it's no fish story.)

One would think that a territory this vast would contain millions of people. It doesn't. The population of Davao is just more than a million. But what the city lacks in numbers it more than makes up for in ethnicity—which is another aspect of Davao's many parts.

Name a Philippine dialect and it is likely to be spoken here. Davao is the quintessential city of immigrants. There are also the region's tribal "natives": the Bagobo, the Manobo, the Mansaka, the B'laan, and the T'boli, all blending in with the other Davaoeños except perhaps on festival days when they put on their native dress. But their crafts—weaving, basketry, brasswork and woodcarvings—as well their music and their dances, continue to give Davao a distinct identity which even mainstreamers have come to claim as their own.

There are other pockets of local color as well. Davao has a substantial Chinese community so it is no surprise that one of the city's grandest landmarks is a Buddhist temple whose priests speak only Mandarin or Fookienese. Then there are the Japanese, remnants of families that came to Davao before the Pacific War and lived in a settlement called Japan Kuo or Little Japan. Most of them are still found in Quintal, the base of their former "government," now a district just outside the city proper. And there are the old Spanish families, which predate everyone else except the indigenous tribes.

Diversity makes for a lively culture, but because of it Davao is yet to find its center. Of course, the city is relatively young compared with other Philippine cities. (Cebu, for instance, is 424 years old and Vigan, 217). Mindanao was the last area to be reorganized politically by the Americans, which is why the province of Davao only dates back to 1914. Its municipal structure wasn't completed until 1937. Then the province was trisected in 1967 into Davao Oriental, Davao del Norte and Davao. And its growth was unplanned, cityhood having been forced on it by circumstance.

CONTRARY TO popular belief, Davao City is not the capital of Davao; Digos is. But it is considered the premier city not only of Davao but also of Davao del Norte and Davao Oriental.

Davao not only has a confused identity, its name is even the subject of confusion. According to one version recorded by the Jesuits from their observations of the Bagobo, Davao derives its name from Daba-Daba, meaning "region of fire." *Dabadaba* was the ancient Bagobo's word for the sacred bush that belonged to a certain Datu Duli, a tribal chief.

In another version, a Monobo rebel named Dabaw founded the region. Others trace Davao to *dabahan*, a big basin used by natives for doing laundry, or to *daba*, a Bagobo earthen pot. Most, however, believe Davao was named after the great river ıt bisects the city, which the Tagbanua call Dava and the iagan refer to as Davoh.

The Bagobo "region of fire" is romantic—although in mod-ı times a bit too descriptive for many Davaoeños. In the 1980s vao lived up to its sobriquet when the NPA used the city as a ›oratory for urban guerrilla warfare. The subsequent rise of Alsa ısa, the anti-communist vigilantes, exacerbated the bloodbath.

These days, though, the fire that makes Davao glow comes ıinly from the flame trees that line the city's highways and from · Davaoeños themselves, who seem to draw heat and en-ıy from living in the Philippines' newest boom town. They know ·ir city is being groomed as the nation's gateway to the East ɜan Growth Polygon.

As to Davao's identity crisis? Perhaps the future holds the an-ɜr as newer immigrants come and help create that elusive nething that will finally put a name to Davao's soul

ACROSS THE ARCHIPELAGO

Have tastebuds, will travel

Eat your way around the Philippines? The proposition is delicious and makes sense too. Food reveals much of a country's history, geography and idiosyncrasies.

Philippine cuisine has all the multiracial features of the Filipino—basically, Malay with a Chinese, Spanish and American underlay. As writer Monina Mercado wryly puts it, we were "first prepared by early Malay settlers, spiced by commercial relations with Chinese traders, stewed in 300 years of Spanish rule and hamburgered by a half-century of American influence." But if you factor in geography, the cuisine enters the realm of the exotic. Native peculiarities rooted in folkways create a food culture comparable to no other.

ANYWHERE THE coconut grows by the hectare, especially in the Tagalog provinces of Southern Luzon and the Bicol Region, anything is a potential *guinataan* dish. Meat, fish, fowl, vegetables are all stewed in fresh coconut milk, making a complete meal. Sweets are similarly cooked. Some sweets, like the all-time favorite concoction of yam, jackfruit, banana and tapioca boiled in sweetened coconut milk, aren't reserved for dessert; they're served with a main dish of salted fish or meat.

In the seaside regions of Luzon, Visayas and Mindanao, the food comes to the table fresh, often straight off the fishing boat and requires the simplest preparation. *Kinilaw*, raw or blanched seafood marinated in vinegar, spices and in some places enriched with coconut milk, is the region's signature dish. One version of *kinilaw* which the Ilocanos of Vigan call "jumping salad" consists of live shrimps swiftly shelled, dipped in vinegar or *kalamansi* and eaten while the animal is still moving. Perhaps not a dish for SPCA members, but surely no worse than wearing a sealskin coat.

Fresh water is the food source in the lakeshore towns. *Kanduli*, a cousin to the catfish, though many swear much tastier, is most often associated with Angono. Folklore says it was the *kanduli* that attracted the town's first settlers, a Bornean *datu* and his clan. As their party was sailing down the Pasig River, prospecting for hospitable land, they spotted crystalline objects shooting out of the water. It was a school of *kanduli*, their white skin glistening in the sun. With an abundance of fish plus the arboreal beauty of Angono, they settled down and settled in. What more could a *datu* or a traveler want?

Thinking about haute cuisine usually means thinking about the French. And when thinking about the French one thinks of sauces. But for fine sauces one doesn't have to dig out a passport. A quick trip to Bulacan and Pampanga is quite sufficient, since Manila's northern neighbors have invented more than 52 different dipping sauces, each intended for a specific dish—tomatoes, salted red eggs and *wansuy* (aromatic coriander) for smoked fish; boiled eggplant and *saba* bananas mixed with vinegar, garlic, pepper and salt for beef putchero; pickled mustard leaves with *tahuri* (soybean paste) braised with finely sliced tomatoes for broiled fish.

The Bulakeños have also created food for the eye. Their unique *pastillas* wrappers are as beautiful as the milky candies are delicious. It is almost a sacrilege to rip up those delicately feligreed paper "tails" cut out to spell "*Mabuhay,*" "*Recuerdo,*" or fashioned into florals and strings of nipa huts.

That food plays a central role in the Pampango's life can be seen in their traditional architecture. The Pampanga grand house seems to be built around the dining room, usually the largest room in the house and in close proximity to the kitchen. In the center of this central room is the dining table, large enough to hold an extended family sitting down to an extended feast. It is never really cleared. On the contrary, it is restocked five times a day—for breakfast, for segunda almuerza or mid-morning snack, for lunch, for merienda or mid-afternoon snack, and for supper. Then as soon as that meal's concluded , fruit and candy dishes materialize for the pleasure of midnight snackers, beginning the cycle anew.

From the Spaniards, the Pampangos learned the European art of preserving and enhancing natural flavors through the use of spices and sauces. Fish, for example, is not merely broiled or boiled like the more spartan Boholanos do. It is stuffed with garlic, tomato and onion, brushed with olive oil, then wrapped in banana leaves before it is cooked over charcoal. Or fried, then simmered in a spicy sauce of vinegar, salt, ginger and sugar, and finally garnished with carrots carved into thin floral morsels.

Up north in the Ilocos Region, the hard land wedged between rugged mountains and the turbulent sea has produced a frugal people whose parsimony extends to their diet. The simplest Ilocano dish is nothing more than boiled vegetables—okra, *ampalaya* and *sayote* shoots—dipped in *bagoong*. Or a less absemious version called *pinakbet*, a medley of vegetables stacked in a pot layer by layer, flavored with a fatty slice of pork and stewed in bagoong. If pork, heaven help the Ilocano, is too expensive fish is substituted and the dish becomes *inabraw.*

Like the Chinese, the Ilocanos eat everything in their midst, especially if it is plucked out of the source and not bought. What others might find exotic—i.e., plant shoots, seaweeds, bee's eggs, and red ants—are common fare, harvested fronm the neighborhood. The exception is garlic, the province's principal crop. The spice is grown to be sold, not to be eaten.

"Waste not, want not," seems to be the motto Ilocanos go by where food is concerned. On special occasions a goat may be slaughtered to enrich the festive table. But every part of the animal goes to the pot: the meaty sections for *caldereta*, the centerpiece dish, a costly stew laden with butter, cheese and olives; the brain and burnt hide are used for *kilawen*, an appetizer; entrails, lungs and heart are thrown into the *sangkutsar*, a soupy dish; the blood becomes the base for *dinuguan*, a hefty stew; the intestines and bile are turned into *papait*, a dish Ilocanos will die for.

The rich Ilocano, however, are as indulgent as rich Filipinos anywhere. They eat unto death, literally. Statistics show that men from the prosperous city of Vigan go to their graves young, their arteries abused by their insatiable palates. Not surprising amongh those raised on a steady diet of *bagnet*, pork skin and belly deep-fried in pork lard; *sinanglaw*, a tart concoction of instestines, tripe and squares of solid blood; Vigan *langgoniza*, spicy pork sausages served with eggs or, when in season, with *ngarosgangis*, tiny shellfish stir-fried in onions and tomatoes.

LIKE ANY nation, the Philippines has developed a reputation for certain flagship dishes such as *adobo*, *pancit* and *lumpia*, both fresh and fried. But travelers going outside the capital region should scan the menu for regional specialties. New foods like new places are part of the discovery process. Here are some suggestions:

Adobong salagubang (beetles) and fried *camaru* (locusts), from Pampanga and Nueva Ecija. Here we have two dishes prepared "American" style, sans the heads, wings and feet. Although the beetle's head is said to be an aphrodisiac, it is tweaked off before it is cooked lest the already raging hormones of the diner get an unwanted booster shot. Gourmets have likened the taste of beetles to boursin cheese and that of *camaru* to the orange fat in the head of a large prawn.

Buro, from Bulacan, Pampanga and Nueva Ecija, is a pungent, odorous side dish made from fermented rice and eaten with broiled fish and steamed vegetables. Unfortunately, many are turned off by the way it looks. In Bulacan and Pampanga, it comes *au naturel*, thus the folk call it *sukang pusa* (cat's vomit). The Novo Ecijano version, however, is gentler on the eyes as it mixed with *angkak* weed, which colors the sauce a reddish pink. Like *balut* (fertilized duck eggs), you have to get used to the *buro*. But once tasted, you'll become addicted.

Pinaupong manok, from Pangasinan, is chicken baked in a claypot lined with salt. Contrary to what's expected, the dish isn't at all salty; just enough salt is used to bring out the fowl's natural flavors. That's because Pangasinan knows all about salt. Saltmaking, a major industry, gave the province its name.

Linambunan, from Cebu, made from a whole fish, usually a red snapper, is marinated in *kalamansi* juice, chili and thick coconut milk and then wrapped and steamed in banana leaves.

Balaw-balaw, from Laguna and other lakeshore towns, is finely chopped shrimps cooked in coconut milk with chilies.

From Iloilo, there are three laboriously prepared dishes travelers should try: *pancit molo*, spiced pork and chicken meat balls daintily wrapped in thin dough and boiled in the chicken and pork broth; La Paz *batchoy*, scissored noodles and pork innards simmered in broth and sprinkled with *chicharon*; and *binakol*, chicken cooked in a bamboo tube.

Ginata-an nga baboy, from Cebu, is pork simmered in coconut milk and seasoned with shrimp fry paste. Another must are *imbao* clams.

Pancit habhab, from Quezon, are noodles and *sayote* sauteed in pork fat and served on banana leaves. Quezon also serves *jardinera*, a dish similar to American meatloaf but better.

Bicol Express is ox skin tenderized in spicy coconut milk, chilies and *bagoong*. As its name implies, the dish makes you run for a glass of water as fast as a nonstop train.

Panga ng tuna, from Davao, is the jaw of the tuna prepared on a charcoal grill. Rich and meaty, some say it is the best section of the gamefish. Tuna fins and tails are also considered tasty, because that's where the fat is concentrated.

Guinataang kasag, from the Visayas, are female crabs simmered in coconut milk. One should also try *Inday-Inday*, a rice cake laced with macapuno.

Adobong manok, Marinduque style. A different approach to the national dish, its ingredients include coconut milk and yellow ginger.

IF YOU are timid about trying new foods, though, we have something else for you, too. McDonald's has outlets throughout the archipelago.

Roadside emporia

You see them on every highway and most secondary roads. Stalls, shops, or often just an open space with merchandise laid out on a blanket. Some have pedestrian names like Bing's Store, some remind the passer-by of close-knit ties (Three Sisters) or boast of a large family (Seven Sisters). Some display ego, such as Superman's, although we're not sure whether the sign refers to a special customer or the owner himself.

Most are *sari-sari* stores or general merchandising outlets for the people who live in the area. But once in a while, you come across a real find—shops that make things or sell things that often wind up in trendy metropolitan boutiques and specialty stores at far higher prices.

Everybody knows about and misses the Betis woodcarvers along the highway to Zambales and Bataan. Lahar put these talented artisans out of business. However, farther up the MacArthur Highway, in Apalit, on the boundary between Bulacan and Pampanga, is the shop of the *pukpok* lady, Ising Ramirez. There, safe from the lahar flow, her workers beat tin into baroque candlesticks, wall moldings, picture frames and mirror frames, all snapped up by Manila antique dealers.

Aling Ising's shop is a lean-to without walls, her showroom is her living room. If you don't like what she already has on display you can ask her to make something else. If she has the pattern, you can have it made while you wait. If not, you can order it. There isn't any price list and she seems a little vague as to what she should charge. We priced a foot-high candlestick embossed with an angel's face. "How much?" we asked. "P400," she replied. Then we saw the same angel's face as a wall hanging. "How much is that?" "P500!" "What?" we asked incredulously, "the candlestick, which is much more elaborate and larger, is only P400." "Okay," she said, "P300." Incidentally, we later saw the same candlestick in an upscale Filipiniana shop in Manila for P1,500.

THE HIGHWAY between Agoo and San Fernando, La Union, is lined on both sides by potter's sheds. Set up on makeshift shelves on the shoulder of the road are flower pots in every size and shape, cooking pots, decorative pots and pots whose function we could only guess at. All the pots are made onsite and decorated by hand.

In Bangar, several towns farther north of San Fernando, every home seems to have a loom. Best buys here are *abel iloco* blankets, pillow cases, tablecloths and monogrammed towels. A personalized blanket for a single bed is only P280, a standard blanket, P250.

The Naguilian public market is the home of homemade *basi*. It is impossible to get good *basi* in Manila, but here, you can wander from stall to stall sampling batches of the sweet purple wine until you find one to your taste. A gallon bottle is under P200.

Farther up in the Cordilleras are the folksy shops. In Banaue there is an entire market filled to the rafters with Ifugao crafts—from *hagabi*, a ritual bench carved out of a single tree trunk, to heirloom blankets whose woven designs chronicle events in the tribe's life. We opted for a rare *bulol*. The Ifugao rice god is commonly depicted as seated on his haunches, elbows resting on his knees and hands cupping his face. Ours, bought for only P700, dances. Its arms are whimsically spread out, looking as if he is priming for a spin.

In Bontoc, the Sunday market is lined with dozens upon dozens of pig's heads. You might suspect there's a guillotine nearby. If you're a vegetarian, you can also get all the fixings for a hearty tossed salad from just one stall.

DOWN IN South Luzon, the roadside pickings are equally plenty. Laguna is *buko* pie country and from Sta. Rosa to Los Banos, street venders and shops hawk the delicious pastry. But which is the best? In this case the store sign says it all, *Original Buko Pie*, and it's located on the road to UP Los Banos, just off the National Highway. On our frequent trips to Makiling, we have bought many of their pies and the crust is always firm and the buko filling, moist. We also like the store's pineapple pies. But what we like best is that in addition to its table-sized pies, they sell miniatures, perfect for eating in the car.

To wash down your pie, there's *lambanog*. It's a weird combination of ingredients, but it works. The provinces of Laguna, Quezon and Batangas sell the potent drink, but be sure to taste it before you buy. We sampled the liquor of several shops until we hit upon the right one somewhere in Lipa, Batangas. If the store has a name, we didn't notice it, but it's near a church and out front are the giant fermenting jars from which the vender, an old lady who looks like she has been pickled in the liquid herself, ladles out the *lambanog* by the gallon. One wonders, though, does the heat sliding down your throat, as you take a sip, come from the *lambanog* or the *Zonrox* bottles they sell it in?

Batangas—along with some Laguna towns like Majayjay—is the place to buy jackknives, gravity knives, and switchblades. The knives—deadly weapons or practical gadgets, depending on how you intend to use them—go by a generic name, *balisong* Batangas, after the lethal temper of the province's menfolk. The quality of the knives runs from crude (good only for "dirty" chores like gardening or splitting a coconut) to sleek (for planting in one's enemy's back). The latter category comes with handles and cases of carabao horn inlaid with bone and brass.

Rizal Avenue in Palawan, going from the airport to downtown Puerto Princesa, has many shops selling native crafts. The merchandise is not only authentic but reasonably priced. Among the items found on this street are native instruments, cooking utensils, spirit boats and carved animals. We bought a *kudyapi* (a two-string lute) for P600, a *rabay* (wild chicken trap) for P150 and several carved snakes for P100 each.

IN THE Visayas, you can go wild. When in Bohol never pass up Tagbilaran, Antiquera and Panglao. Tagbilaran's antique shops can furnish your entire house, from *capiz* windows to brass conversation pieces engraved with *mata-mata*, or eye motif. The Sunday market in Antiquera is a warren of stalls selling baskets, mats and all types of products hand-woven from reed, *nito*, rattan and bamboo. Any day in Duljo, Panglao, is a day for the shell market on the beach of this seaside barrio. There are golden cowries, tritons, melon shells, volutes, conches and spindles, enough to turn you into an instant collector. But if food is your trip, Duljo is the cheapest place to gorge on *uni* (called *suaki* in the local dialect). The heavenly roe of sea urchins is sold for P20 a bottle or less than the price of one piece of *uni* sushi at any Japanese restaurant in Metro Manila.

In Negros Occidental, delicacies range from truly fresh—as in *biscocho* just taken out of a traditional oven—or truly petrified—as in leathery but tasty dried *tanguige*.

Wayside stalls in Samar teem with prawns and crabs so fresh they seem to have just crawled out of the ponds along the coastal highway. Samar also produces beautiful sleeping mats made of *pandan*. Purists may scorn these mats since the designs are inserted over the basic ground rather than directly woven, but when you see the complex landscapes (i.e., florals or the map of the Philippines) which cover three square meters, you can't help but marvel at the accurate reproduction. In the neighboring province of Leyte, mat weavers produce photographic portraits or scenes. Unless you have the time to have your own face done, settle for next best thing—the spectacle of San Juanico Bridge which joins the islands of Samar and Leyte rendered in great detail (including the bridge's shadow), a wonderful example of folk art.

WHAT ABOUT Mindanao? Take any road in Davao and it will eventually lead to a fruit stall where mangosteen, *rambutan*, pomelo and *durian* can be had for less than half of what they cost in Manila. Next to fruits, Davao is known for its flower orchards where cut orchids go for a song. Since the province is a melting pot of ethnic groups, its markets abound with craft from the various tribes—Maguindanao, Bagobo, Mandaya and T'boli. The last two have their own craft centers. The Mandaya Weaving Center is run by a tribal blue blood. The T'boli Center, tended by costumed natives, is a treasure trove where finds can be as fanciful as bamboo paper clips (would you believe P1 for a set of 12?) and horsehair earrings (P70 a pair) to the elegant T'boli cloth (P300 per yard) and T'boli jacket (P1,500).

In Zamboanga, the barter markets burst with canned goods and *sotanghon* from China, *batik* from Indonesia, temple rubbings from Thailand, "blue seal" cigarettes from Malaysia and other imported items. But our favorites are the Yakan Weaving center by the coastal road and the floating market at the back of Lantaka Hotel by the sea. The Yakan turn out yards and yards of their elegant cloth. Not cheap, but certainly cheaper than anywhere else. On a trip to the Museum of Natural History in New York we browsed at the museum shop and found reason to gloat. They were selling a piece of Yakan cloth measuring about two yards for $700; we got ours, a longer one too, in Zamboanga for only P900. The bancas at the floating market are laden with shells, corals, brassware, food covers and trays of dyed palm and *laminusa* mats. When it comes to mats, nothing can beat the *laminusa*, except the mats from Ungos Matata in Cagayan de Sulu, which are woven exclusively for the family's use. The *laminusa* is a riot of contrasting colors defining geometric lines—sawtooths, triangles, squares and so on. Its overall look resembles Op Art though it predates the genre by hundreds of years.

SOMETIMES YOU get unintended bargains. A friend was complaining that he needed a dress watch for the very few occasions that require one. So rather than spend a lot of money on something he would use just once in while, he decided to play tourist and took a walk down M.H. del Pilar. It didn't take more than a few steps before he was offered a Rolex, which looked fine except that the name on the watch face was spelled Rollex. P500 was asked and P120 accepted. We wonder if that "street vender" would be disappointed to know that the Rollex is still telling time.